The McGraw-Hill
Big Book
of
Science
Activities

The McGraw-Hill
Big Book
of
Science
Activities

Fun and Easy Experiments for Kids

Robert W. Wood

McGraw-Hill

New York   San Francisco   Washington, D.C.   Auckland   Bogotá
Caracas   Lisbon   London   Madrid   Mexico City   Milan
Montreal   New Delhi   San Juan   Singapore
Sydney   Tokyo   Toronto

Library of Congress Cataloging-in-Publication Data applied for.

McGraw-Hill

A Division of The McGraw·Hill Companies

2 3 4 5 6 7 8 9 0   DOC/DOC   0 4 3 2 1 0

ISBN 0-07-071873-3

The sponsoring editor for this book was Griffin Hansbury, the development
editor was Mary Loebig Giles, the editing supervisor was Patricia V. Amoroso,
and the production supervisor was Clare B. Stanley. It was set in Garamond by
Dennis Smith of McGraw-Hill's Professional Book Group composition unit.

Printed and bound by R. R. Donnelley & Sons Company.

McGraw-Hill books are available at special quantity discounts to use as
premiums and sales promotions, or for use in corporate training programs. For
more information, please write to the Director of Special Sales, McGraw-Hill,
Professional Publishing, Two Penn Plaza, New York, NY 10121-2298. Or contact
your local bookstore.

This book was printed on recycled, acid-free paper containing a
minimum of 50% recycled de-inked fiber.

Contents

Part II   Chemistry   77

Part III Meteorology 139

Part IV Geology 203

Part V   Animal Biology   263

Part VI Plant Biology   343

Part VII Engineering   399

Introduction

This book consists of seven parts introducing geography, chemistry, meteorology, geology, animal biology, plant biology, and engineering.

Science is a subject that becomes instantly exciting with even the simplest discoveries. On any day, and at any time, we can see these mysteries unfold around us.

This book was written to open the door, and to invite, the curious to enter—to explore, to think, and to wonder. To realize that anyone, absolutely anyone at all, can experiment and learn. To discover that the only thing you really need to study science is an inquiring mind. The rest of the material is all around you. It is there for anyone to see. You have only to look.

Be sure to read the How to Use This Book section that follows before you begin any experiments. It warns you of all the safety precautions you should consider before you begin a project and whether or not you should have a teacher, parent, or other adult help you.

Completely read through a project before you begin to be sure you understand the experiment and you have all of the materials you'll need. Each experiment has a materials list and easy, step-by-step instructions with illustrations to help you.

Although you will want to pick a project that interests you, you might want to do the experiments in order. It isn't necessary, but some of the principles you learn in the first few experiments will provide you with some basic understanding and help you do the later experiments.

Finally, keep safety in mind, and you are sure to have a rewarding first experience in the exciting world of science.

How to Use This Book

All of the experiments in this book can be done safely, but young children should be instructed to respect fire and the hazards associated with carelessness. The following symbols are used throughout the book for you to use as a guide to what children might be able to do independently and what they *should not do* without adult supervision. Keep in mind that some children might not be mature enough to do any of the experiments without adult help, and that these symbols should be used as a guide only and do not replace the good judgment of parents or teachers.

 Materials or tools used in this experiment could be dangerous in young hands. Adult supervision is recommended. Children should be instructed on the care and handling of sharp tools or combustible or toxic materials and how to protect surfaces.

 Protective gloves that are flame retardant and heat resistant should be worn. Handling hot objects and hot wax can burn hands. Protect surfaces beneath hot materials—do not set pots of boiling water or very hot objects directly on tabletops or counters. Use towels or heat pads.

Protective safety goggles should be worn during each experiment to protect against shattering glass or other hazards that could damage the eyes. Keep in mind that in chemical laboratories, for example, workers wear safety goggles at all times—regardless of the specific experiment.

 Flame or another heat source is used in this project and adult supervision is required. Do not wear loose clothing. Tie hair back. When handling candles, wear protective gloves—hot wax can burn. Never leave a flame or a source of heat unattended. Extinguish flame properly. Protect surfaces beneath burning candles.

 The use of the stove, boiling water, or other hot materials are used in this project and adult supervision is required. Keep other small children away from boiling water and burners.

 Electricity is used in this experiment. Young children should be supervised and older children cautioned about the hazards of electricity.

PART I

GEOGRAPHY

1

Map of the Earth

Look at the map of the earth and you will notice that the North Pole is at the top and the South Pole is at the bottom (Fig. 1-1). You also can see that it is divided in the middle by the equator (Fig. 1-2). The map is further divided by lines running up and down and lines running from left to right, or around the globe. Map makers draw these lines to help us find directions, the time, and the seasons. The lines running up and down all come together at the North Pole and the South Pole. These are the lines of longitude (Fig. 1-3). The lines running across the map from left to right are the lines of latitude (Fig. 1-4). They are divided by the equator. The areas of the earth north of the equator have winter in January and summer in July. The areas south of the equator have opposite seasons—winter in July and summer in January (Fig. 1-5).

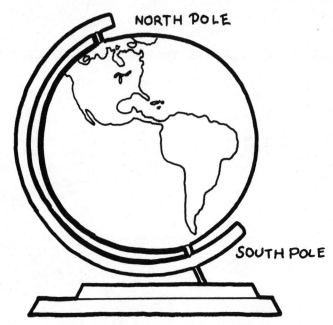

Fig. 1-1. *A globe is a spherical model of the earth that shows the continents and the seas.*

Fig 1-2. *The earth is divided around the middle by the equator.*

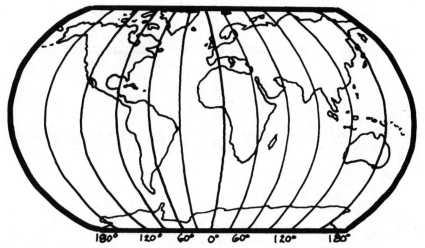

Fig. 1-3. *The lines that run from the North Pole to the South Pole are the lines of longitude.*

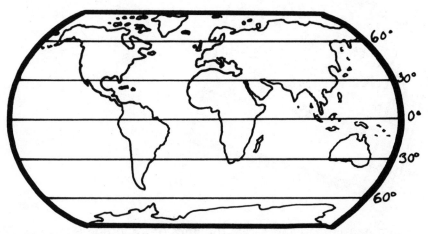

Fig. 1-4. *The lines that run from east to west are the lines of latitude.*

Fig. 1-5. *The areas that are divided by the equator have opposite seasons.*

2
Longitude and the Prime Meridian

Materials

- MAP OR GLOBE
- WATCH
- 2 STRAIGHT STICKS (ABOUT 12 INCHES LONG)
- HAMMER
- MAGNETIC COMPASS

Examine the map and locate the lines of longitude (Fig. 2-1). Find the 0 degree longitude line. It runs through Greenwich Observatory, near London (Fig. 2-2). This observatory marks the prime meridian of the earth. World time is calculated from this point. It is measured at the instant the sun passes directly over the observatory. Locations can be found by counting the longitude east and west from this imaginary line. The distance between the degrees becomes smaller as the lines of longitude approach the North Pole. For example, 1 degree longitude along the southern United States is about 60 miles wide, while 1 degree longitude across southern Canada is less than 45 miles wide (Fig. 2-3).

In a sunny area outside, and just before noon, draw a line in the dirt running north and south (Fig. 2-4). Drive the two sticks straight into the ground on this line. Watch the shadows of both sticks (Fig. 2-5). When the two shadows are in line, the sun will be passing through its highest point (Fig. 2-6). This is the meridian, or longitude, of your location.

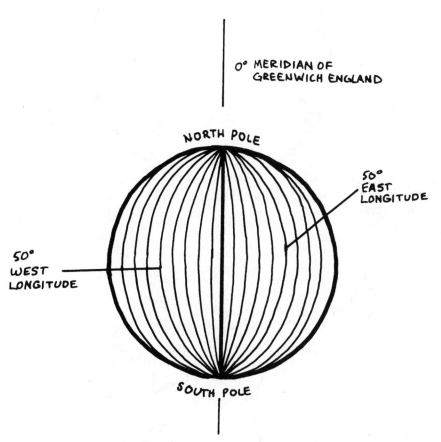

Fig. 2-1. *The lines of longitude are measured east and west from the 0 degree longitude line.*

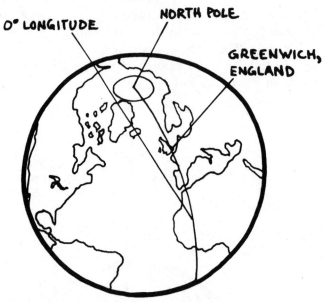

Fig. 2-2. *The 0 degree longitude line, or prime meridian, runs through Greenwich, England.*

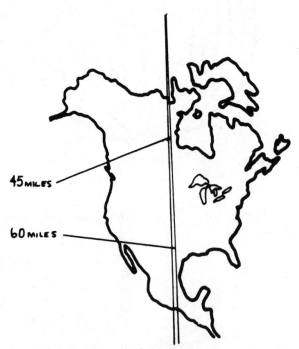

Fig. 2-3. *The distance between the degrees longitude becomes smaller as they approach the North and South Poles.*

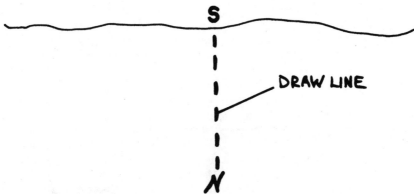

Fig. 2-4. *Scratch a line in the dirt that runs north and south.*

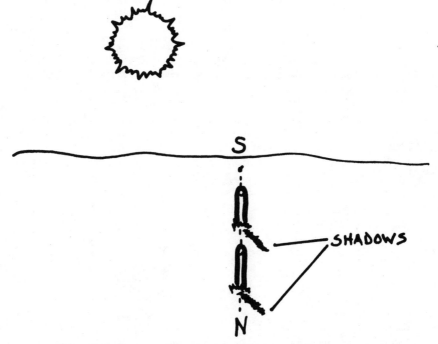

Fig. 2-5. *Notice the shadows that are created by the sticks.*

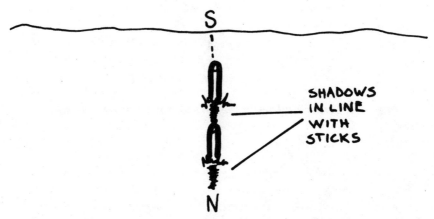

S

SHADOWS
IN LINE
WITH
STICKS

N

Fig. 2-6. *When the shadows are in line, they mark the longitude of your location.*

3

Finding North by the Sun

Materials

- SUNNY DAY
- STRAIGHT STICK (ABOUT 12 INCHES LONG)
- HAMMER

Drive the stick into the ground at an angle that points straight at the sun (Fig. 3-1). The stick should not make a shadow. Wait about an hour, or until the stick casts a shadow about 6 inches long. The shadow will be pointing east from the stick (Fig. 3-2). The sun has now moved toward the west. If you stand with your right shoulder pointing in the direction of the shadow (east), you will be facing north (Fig. 3-3).

Fig. 3-1. Drive the stick into the ground at an angle directly at the sun.

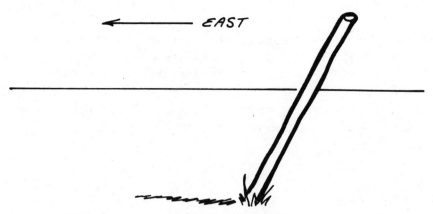

Fig. 3-2. The stick will cast a shadow that points east.

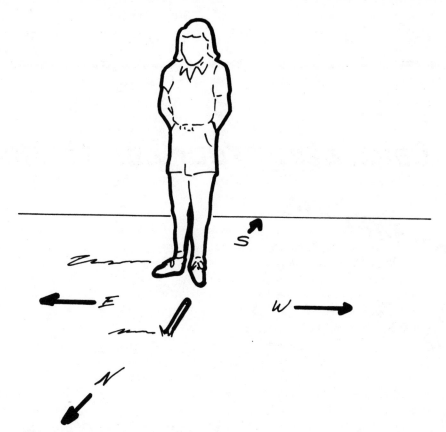

Fig. 3-3. *Point your right shoulder with the shadow and you will be facing north.*

4

Calculating Your Longitude

Materials

- MAP
- WATCH

Find the lines of longitude on the map. Locate the prime meridian, the 0 degree longitude line (Fig. 4-1).

There are 360 degrees in the earth's circumference. Because the earth turns once on its axis every 24 hours, 15 degrees of longitude pass beneath the sun each hour (Fig. 4-2). For each 15 degrees west of Greenwich, the time is set back one hour. For each 15 degrees east of Greenwich, the time is advanced one hour.

Find the line of longitude nearest your location. If you live along a line running from New Orleans north through St. Louis you might find a longitude of 90 degrees (Fig. 4-3). For example, the suburbs of Memphis lie across the 90 degree longitude line (Fig. 4-4). If you divide 90 degrees by 15 degrees, you can see that your location is about 6 hours from Greenwich. So if you know the Greenwich time (also called universal time or U.T.), and you know the time where you are, you can easily calculate your longitude. For example, if it is noon in Greenwich, and 6:00 AM where you are, you would have a longitude of 90 degrees west (Fig. 4-5).

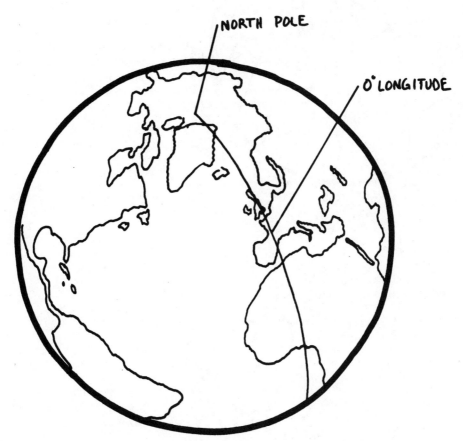

Fig. 4-1. *Find the prime meridian on the globe.*

NORTH POLE

Fig. 4-2. *Fifteen degrees of longitude pass beneath the sun every hour.*

90°

ST. LOUIS • CHICAGO
• MEMPHIS
• NEW ORLEANS

Fig. 4-3. *The 90 degree longitude line that runs through North America.*

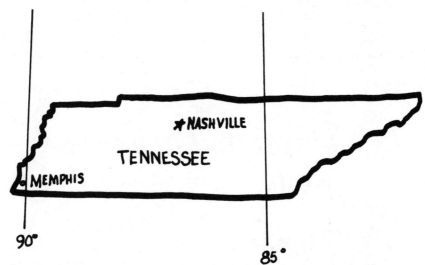

Fig. 4-4. *The 90 degree longitude line passes through the suburbs of Memphis, Tennessee.*

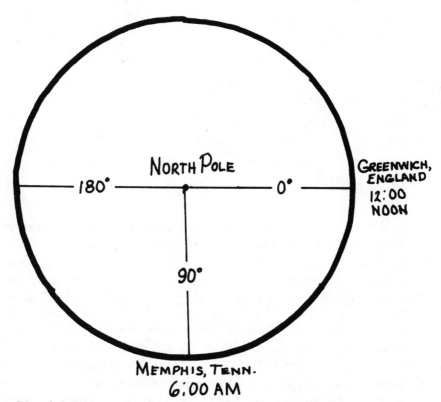

Fig. 4-5. *When it is twelve noon at Greenwich, England, it is 6:00 AM along the 90 degree line of longitude.*

5
Lines of Latitude

Materials

• WORLD MAP OR GLOBE

Examine the map and locate the lines of latitude. As the lines of longitude begin with 0 degrees at Greenwich, the lines of latitude begin with 0 degrees at the equator. They are measured north and south to 90 degrees at the poles (Fig. 5-1). Latitude, like longitude is measured in degrees. The North Pole has a latitude of 90 degrees north. The South Pole has a latitude of 90 degrees south. The length of 1 degree latitude is about 69 statute (land) miles (Fig. 5-2). Degrees are further divided into 60 parts called minutes (Fig. 5-3). The minutes are divided into 60 seconds. These are distance measurements, not time. When giving locations, latitude is read first, then longitude. If we had a location of 34 degrees north latitude and 118 degrees, 30 minutes west longitude, we would be just off the beach of Santa Monica, California (Fig. 5-4).

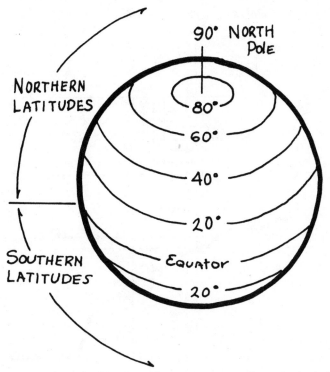

Fig. 5-1. *The lines of latitude are measured north and south from the equator.*

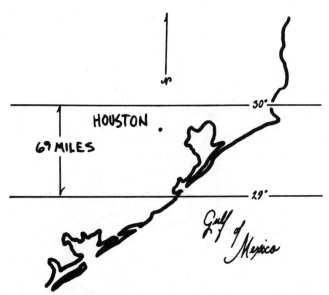

Fig. 5-2. *The length of 1 degree latitude is about 69 miles.*

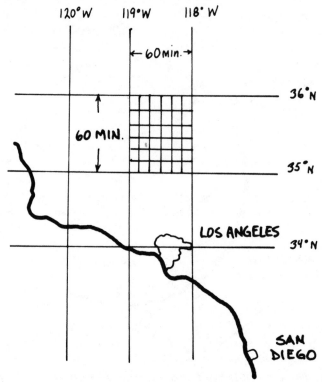

Fig. 5-3. *Degrees are divided into 60 parts called minutes.*

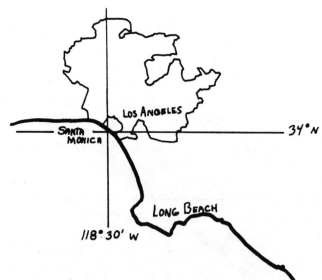

Fig. 5-4. *Thirty-four degrees north and 118 degrees, 30 minutes west is a location near Santa Monica, California.*

6
Finding the North Star

The North Star is easy to find on a clear night. Simply face the northern half of the sky and locate the Big Dipper. The Big Dipper is a group of seven bright stars that look like the side view of a pan with a handle (Fig. 6-1). The Big Dipper moves in a circle around the North Star. In the winter, the handle of the dipper will be pointing down (Fig. 6-2). In the spring, the dipper will be upside down (Fig. 6-3). In the summer, the handle will be pointing up (Fig. 6-4). In the autumn, the dipper will be rightside up (Fig. 6-5).

Notice the two bright stars in the front of the dipper. These are the two stars farthest from the handle. They point to the North Star and are called the pointer stars. Estimate the distance between these two stars. Count about five of these spaces on a line from the end of the Big Dipper, and you should find the North Star. The North Star is also the end star in the handle of the Little Dipper.

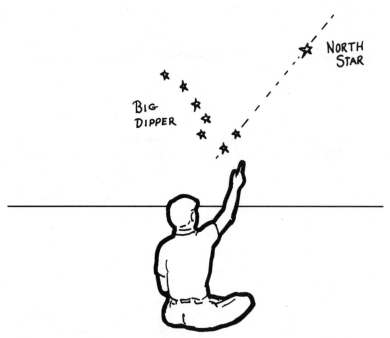

Fig. 6-1. *To find the North Star, face the northern half of the sky and look for the Big Dipper.*

Fig. 6-2. *In winter, the handle of the Big Dipper will be pointing down.*

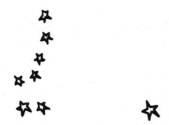

Fig. 6-3. *In the spring, the Big Dipper will be upside down.*

Fig. 6-4. *In the summer, the handle of the Big Dipper will be pointing up.*

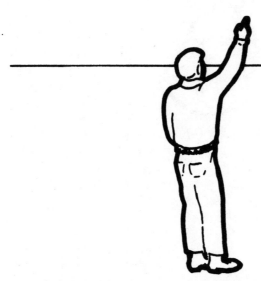

Fig. 6-5. *In the autumn, the Big Dipper will be rightside up.*

7

Finding Your Latitude from the North Star

Materials
- 1 PIECE OF POSTER BOARD (ABOUT 5 x 5 INCHES)
- PLASTIC DRINKING STRAW
- STRING (ABOUT 8 INCHES LONG)
- PAPER CLIP
- SMALL WEIGHT

Materials
(SINKER, WASHER, ETC.)
- SCOTCH TAPE
- PROTRACTOR
- PENCIL
- SCISSORS

Draw a line on two sides of the posterboard 1/2 inch from the edge (Fig. 7-1). Place the protractor as shown in Fig. 7-2 and mark the angles, from 0 to 90 degrees, on the posterboard. Mark off and label the degrees in units of 10; 0, 10, 20, 30, etc. Make a smaller mark halfway between to represent each 5 degrees; 5, 15, 25, etc. Trim off the excess part of the card (Fig. 7-3). Punch a small hole where the lines meet and thread one end of the string through this hole. Tie the end of the string to the paper clip to keep the string from slipping back through. Tie the weight to the other end of the string. Next, tape the straw to the top edge of the card—the edge closest to where the lines meet and the 90 degree mark. When you sight the North Star through the straw, the string will mark the degree of latitude of your location (Fig. 7-4).

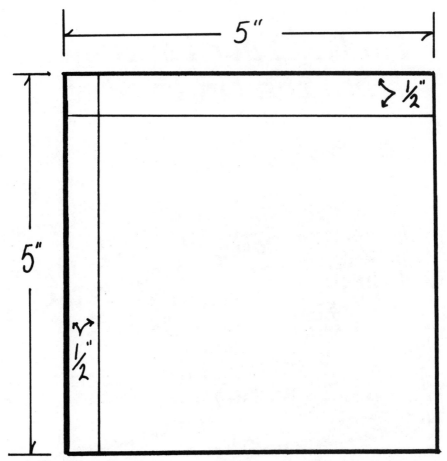

Fig. 7-1. *Draw lines ¹/2 inch from the edge of the posterboard.*

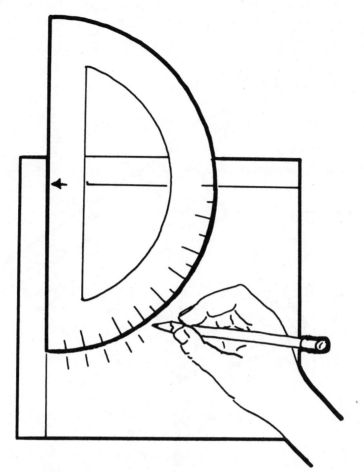

Fig. 7-2. *Mark the angles from 0 to 90 degrees.*

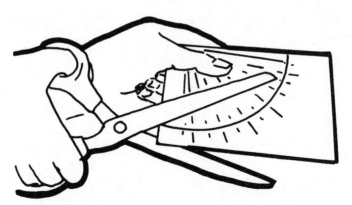

Fig. 7-3. *Cut the excess material from the card.*

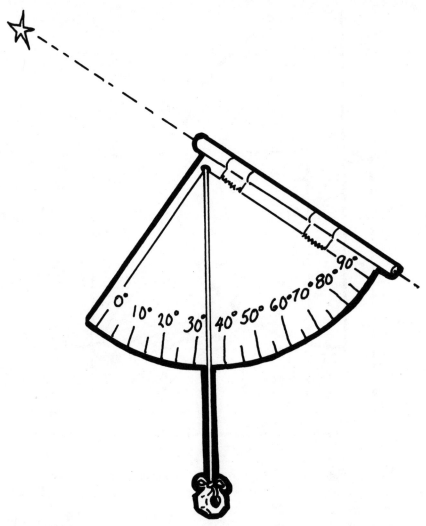

Fig. 7-4. *Sight through the straw at the North Star to find your degree of latitude.*

8
Shadows on a Map

Because most maps are flat, there had to be some way of showing the steepness of mountains. Map makers use a series of lines drawn close together to create the effect of shadows.

Make several folds in the paper something like an accordion (Fig. 8-1). Unfold the paper, and place it flat on a table. Position the flashlight above the upper corner of the paper (Fig. 8-2). Let the light shine across the paper.

Shadows will appear on one side of the folds (Fig. 8-3). The shadows are wide and show a shallow slope. Push the paper together from the ends. Notice how the shadows show steepness (Fig. 8-4). You can see how the shadows on a flat map show the slope of mountains.

Fig. 8-1. Fold the paper into sections.

Fig. 8-2. Place the flashlight near an upper corner.

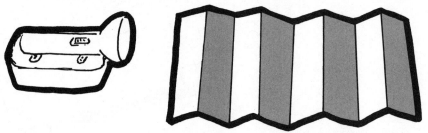

Fig. 8-3. The light will cast shadows on the folds.

Fig. 8-4. Push the paper together to create steeper shadows.

9

Mountains and Contour Lines

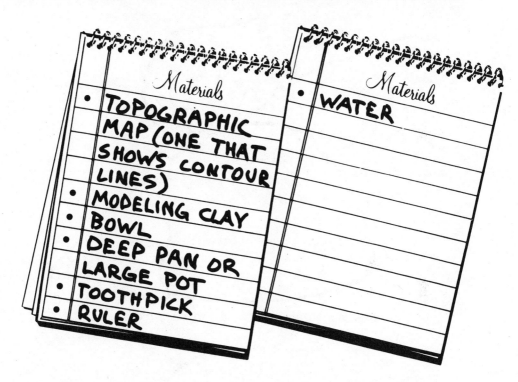

Materials
- TOPOGRAPHIC MAP (ONE THAT SHOWS CONTOUR LINES)
- MODELING CLAY
- BOWL
- DEEP PAN OR LARGE POT
- TOOTHPICK
- RULER

Materials
- WATER

Examine the map and you will notice a pattern of lines. These are contour lines. A contour line connects all points of the same elevation at a particular area.

Turn the bowl upside down and place it on a flat surface. Apply the modeling clay to the outside of the bowl (Fig. 9-1). Shape the clay in the form of a small mountain. The bowl is just to be a base for the mountain. Cover the bowl completely (Fig. 9-2). Place the mountain into the pot. Stand the ruler next to the mountain and pour in one inch of water (Fig. 9-3). Use the toothpick to draw a line around the mountain at the edge of the water (Fig. 9-4). This is a contour line. Pour in another inch of water. Mark another line around the mountain. Continue adding the same amount of water, and marking lines until you reach the top of the mountain. Remove the mountain from the water and place it on a flat surface. Look down at the mountain from directly over its center (Fig. 9-5). You will see how contour lines show the shape of a mountain. Where the lines are close together, the slope is steeper. The numbers in the lines represent the elevation of the lines. In Fig. 9-6, the space between contours is 10, with the elevation at 650. The units can represent feet or meters, depending on the map.

Fig. 9-1. *Apply clay to the outside of the bowl.*

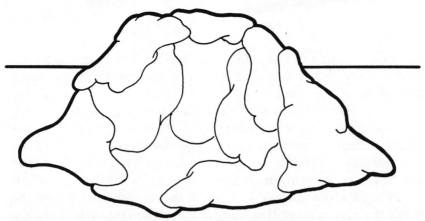

Fig. 9-2. *Cover the bowl completely and shape it into the form of a mountain.*

Fig. 9-3. *Use the ruler to measure 1 inch of water.*

Fig. 9-4. *Use the toothpick to mark the water line.*

Fig. 9-5. *Contour lines show the shape of the mountain.*

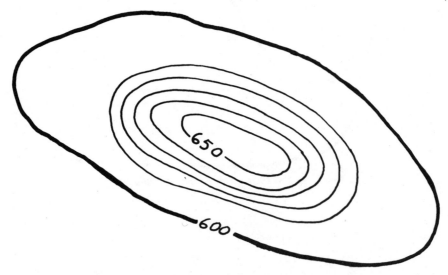

650

600

Fig. 9-6. *The elevation of this mountain is 650.*

10
Depression Contours

Stand the ruler in the bowl and pour in one inch of water. Use the pencil to mark the edge of the water line. This is a contour line. Add another inch of water and mark another line. Continue adding water and marking lines until the bowl is full. Empty the water and look straight down at the lines. You can see contour lines that show the shape of the bowl (Fig. 10-1). Imagine the bowl is sunk in the ground, but on a map this would look just like a hill. To avoid confusion, map makers show depressions with depression contours (Fig. 10-2). These depression contours have short lines on one side of the contour lines. These short lines point downslope. You can mark small lines inside the bowl to show that it is a depression. In the illustration, the contour interval is 10. The top of the hole is at 600, whereas the bottom elevation is 570 (Fig. 10-3).

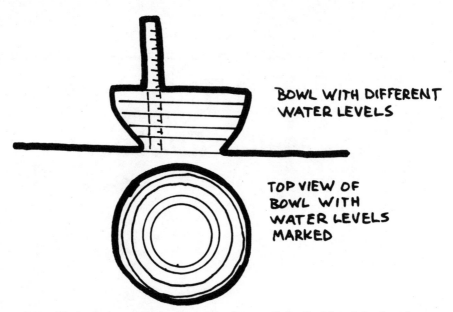

BOWL WITH DIFFERENT WATER LEVELS

TOP VIEW OF BOWL WITH WATER LEVELS MARKED

Fig. 10-1. *Contour lines show the shape of the inside of the bowl.*

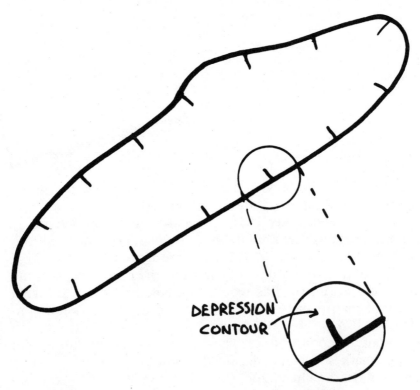

DEPRESSION CONTOUR

Fig. 10-2. *Illustration of a depression contour line.*

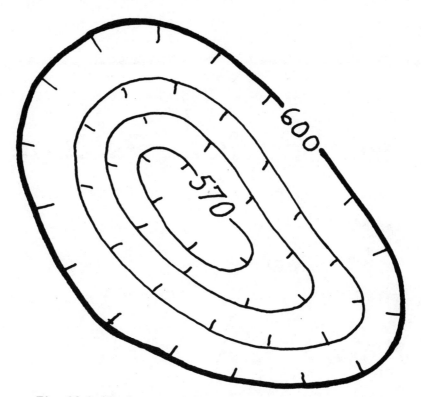

Fig. 10-3. *The bottom of this hole has an elevation of 570.*

11
Plotting Slope Patterns

Look at the map and find the contour line that represents a hill. Place the sheet of paper across the center of the hill. Use the ruler to measure units of 10 straight up on the paper, and on line with each contour line. These units represent elevation. The first contour line represents the bottom of the hill, so begin measuring from the second line. Make a small dot at each elevation (Fig. 11-1). Connect the dots and you will have a rough pattern of the slope of the hill (Fig. 11-2).

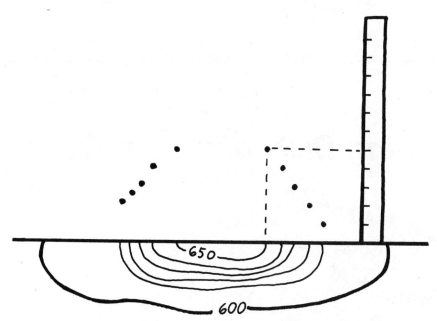

Fig. 11-1. *Use a ruler to make the dots for each elevation.*

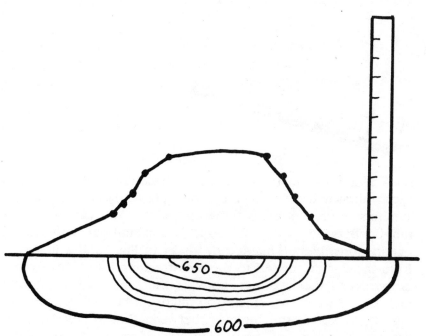

Fig. 11-2. *Connect the dots to show a rough pattern of the slope of the hill.*

12

Reading Distance on a Road Map

Materials

• ROAD MAP

Look at the road map and locate the legend, or key, that displays the symbols that are used on the map (Fig. 12-1). Notice one of the symbols represents miles between points. You can see a large number between two stars. This is the total mileage between cities or junctions that are marked by a star. In Fig. 12-2, it is 60 miles from the star on the left to the crossroad, and 30 miles from the crossroad to the next star. Look at the road map and select a highway between two cities. You might find something similar to Fig. 12-3. Notice the highway between Smith City and Bitter Springs. The numbers on the left side of the road represent the number of miles between the towns along the highway. Starting at Smith City; 17 miles to The Gap, 8 miles to Cedar Ridge, and 18 miles to Bitter Springs. The larger number on the right side of the highway represents the miles between Smith City and Bitter Springs—the cities marked by the stars. Map makers have provided an easy way to find the mileage without doing any measuring.

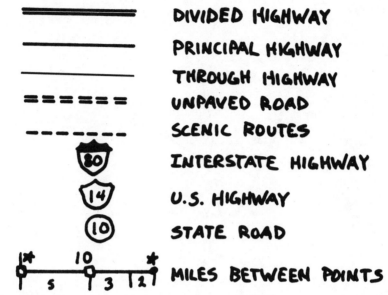

Fig. 12-1. The legend identifies the symbols that are used on the map.

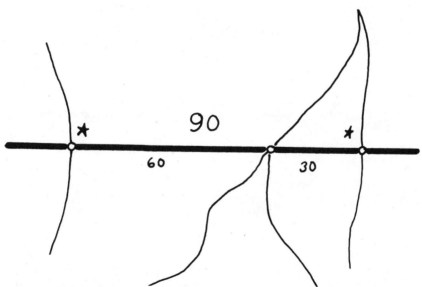

Fig. 12-2. The larger number between the two stars represents the total mileage between the two stars.

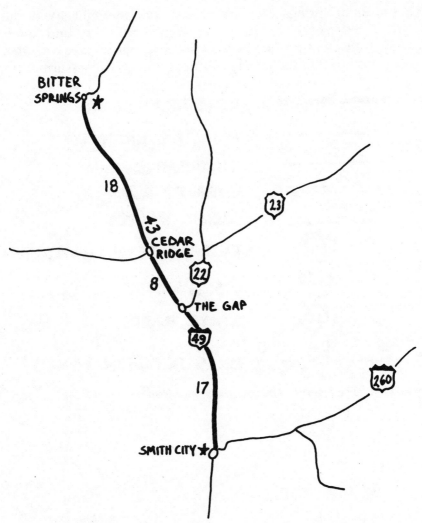

Fig. 12-3. It is 43 miles between Smith City and Bitter Springs.

13
Measuring Distance

Look at the map and find the legend. There should be a line, or lines, representing the scale of miles. It should look something like Fig. 13-1. (The illustrations in this book are for examples only and are not to scale.) Notice the number of miles that are covered in one inch. You have some idea of distance just by estimating the number of inches. To be more accurate, spread the map on a flat surface and place the end of the ruler at the point you want to measure from (Fig. 13-2). Roads seldom run straight for long so you will have to turn the ruler to follow the road (Fig. 13-3). Measure as accurately as you can to the other point. When you know the total number of inches between the two points, multiply by the number of miles per inch to get the distance.

If you don't have a ruler, use the straight edge of a piece of paper. Make a mark at the starting point, turn the paper to follow the road, and make a mark at the destination (Fig. 13-4). If one edge of the paper is not long enough, use the other side. Place the edge of the paper next to the scale of miles on the map, and calculate the distance.

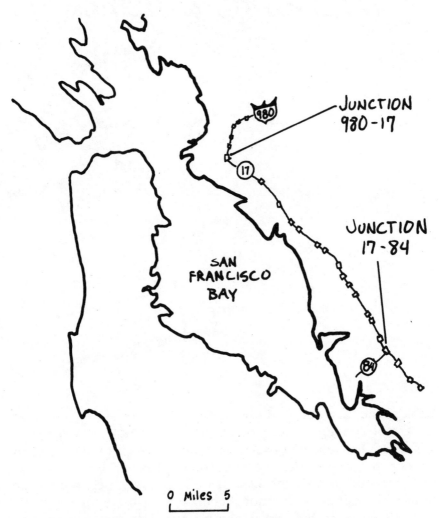

Fig. 13-1. *The map has a line that represents the scale of miles.*

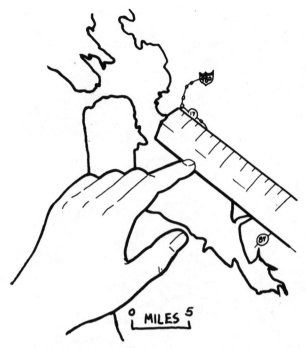

Fig. 13-2. *Use a ruler to measure the distance.*

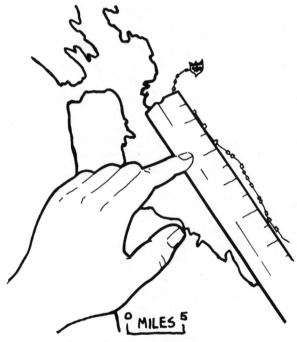

Fig. 13-3. *Turn the ruler to follow the road.*

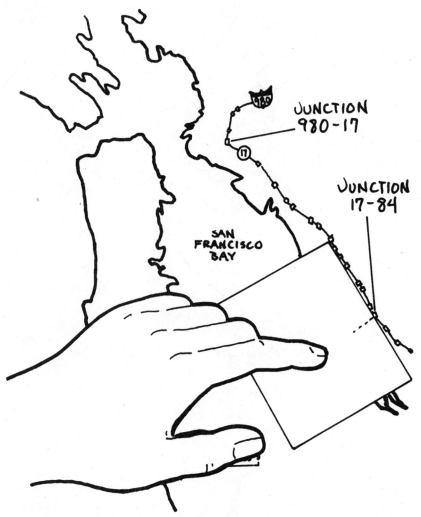

Fig. 13-4. *The straight edge of a piece of paper can be used to measure the distance.*

14
Calculating Range

Materials
- ROAD MAP
- STRING

Imagine a typical car that has a 15-gallon fuel tank. You don't want to run it dry, so you might choose 12 gallons as usable fuel for traveling. If the car gets about 20 miles for each gallon of fuel used, you can see you have a range of about 240 miles. Place the map on a flat surface. Tie a knot in one end of the string. Find the scale of miles on the map and place the knot at the 0 mark. Stretch the string along the scale of miles and measure 240 miles. Tie another knot at this point (Fig. 14-1). Hold the first knot on your location. Stretch the string out across the map to find the range of your car (Fig. 14-2). Remember that you can't usually drive from one place to another in a straight line so you have to reduce the range to compensate. This method will give you a reasonably accurate range for an aircraft.

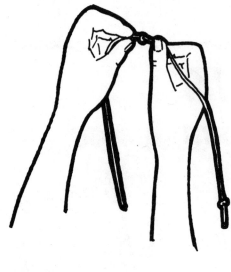

Fig. 14-1. *Tie a knot in the string to represent the range.*

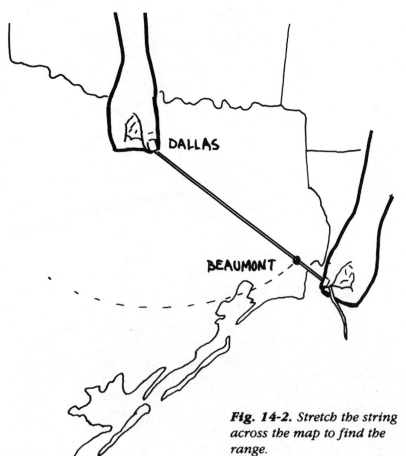

DALLAS

BEAUMONT

Fig. 14-2. *Stretch the string across the map to find the range.*

15
Orientating a Map

Spread the map on a flat surface, and imagine it as a flat, shrunken model of the landscape. Find your location on the map. Assume you wanted to go from your house to a place you had never been to before, a city park, for example. You find the park on the map, and you see the direction from your house. Plot the route on the map (Fig. 15-1). You might have to turn right on one street, or left on another. Transfer the directions from the map to the landscape. Line up the streets on the map with the streets where you live (Fig. 15-2). You are orientating the map with the landscape. You might have to read the map upside down, or sideways. If you need to go right on the map to get to the park, it will be right on the landscape. Most maps have the top of the map pointing north.

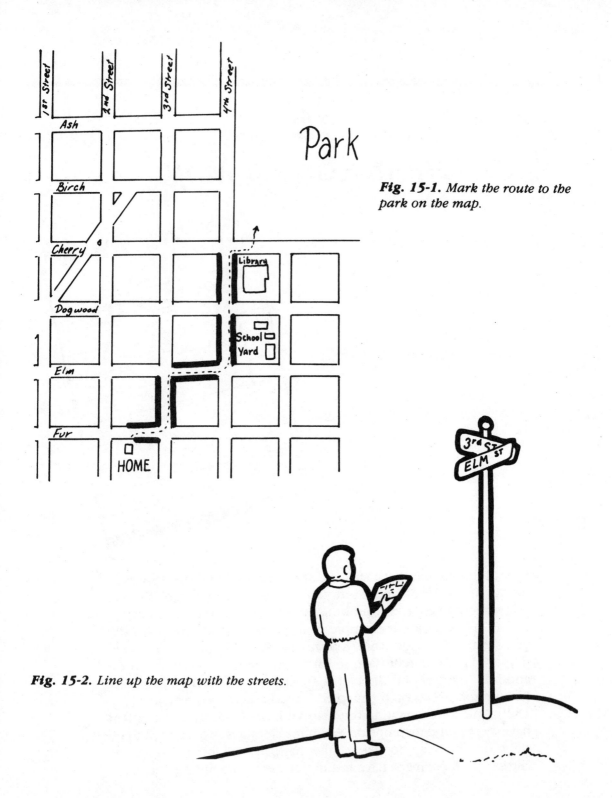

Fig. 15-1. Mark the route to the park on the map.

Fig. 15-2. Line up the map with the streets.

16
Making a Compass

Materials

- MAGNET
- STEEL NEEDLE
- FINE THREAD (ABOUT 8 INCHES LONG)
- WOODEN PENCIL
- DRINKING GLASS
- SMALL PIECE OF PAPER (ABOUT 1×2 INCHES)

Fold the paper in half to make a 1-inch square. Thread the needle and tie a knot at the end of the thread. The knot is to keep the thread from pulling through the paper. Open the folded paper a little and push the needle through the center from the inside of the fold (Fig. 16-1). Carefully pull the needle through the paper stopping when the knot reaches the paper. Remove the thread from the needle and tie the free end of the thread around the middle of the pencil. The length of thread should suspend the pencil approximately an inch above the bottom of the glass. Magnetize the needle by stroking it about 20 times with one end of the magnet. With the paper spread tentlike, insert the needle horizontally through both sides of the paper (Fig. 16-2). Center the needle so that it will balance. Lower the needle into the glass so that it is free to turn. The needle will swing a few times, and then it will align itself north and south (Fig. 16-3).

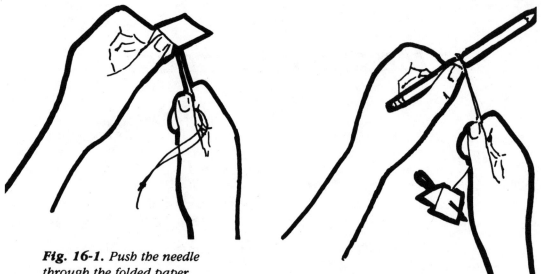

Fig. 16-1. *Push the needle through the folded paper.*

Fig. 16-2. *Tie the thread to the pencil.*

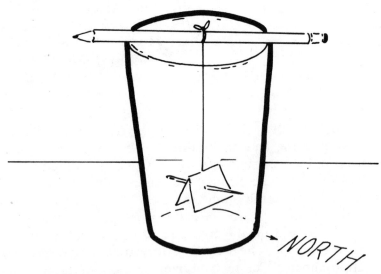

Fig. 16-3. *One end of the needle will point north.*

17
Magnetic Deviation

Materials
- MAGNETIC COMPASS
- HAMMER (ANY PIECE OF IRON)

Place the compass on a flat surface and allow the needle to settle in one direction (Fig. 17-1). Slowly bring the head of the hammer near the needle. Watch the needle change directions (Fig. 17-2). Iron or steel objects brought near a magnetic compass will cause the needle to give false readings.

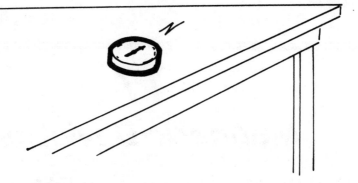

Fig. 17-1. *Place the compass on a flat surface.*

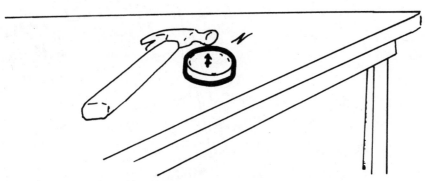

Fig. 17-2. *Magnetic deviation is the deflection of a compass needle due to outside influences such as iron or steel.*

18
North and Magnetic North

Examine the area of the earth near the top of the map. You can see that the North Pole is at the top where all the lines of longitude come together. However, the magnetic North Pole is further south, near Prince Of Wales Island in Canada (Fig. 18-1). It is roughly at 75 degrees north latitude, and 100 degrees west longitude. Because the magnetic axis of the earth is not the same as the true north and south axis, magnetic compasses rarely point true north. The angle between the true North Pole and the magnetic North Pole is called the *angle of magnetic declination*, or *variation* (Fig. 18-2). The magnetic North Pole tends to drift somewhat, causing these angles to change. Charts that show magnetic declination angles must be upgraded every few years.

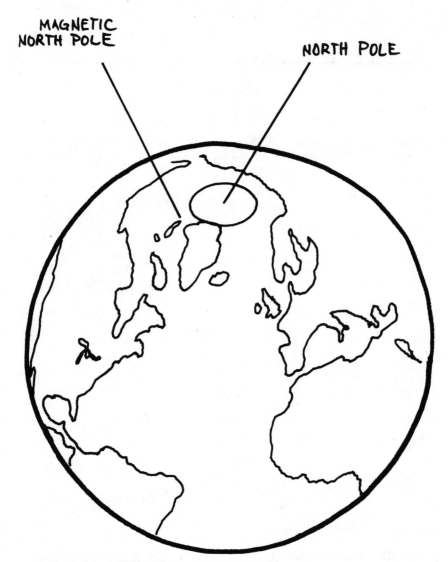

MAGNETIC
NORTH POLE

NORTH POLE

Fig. 18-1. *Magnetic North Pole is south of the true North Pole.*

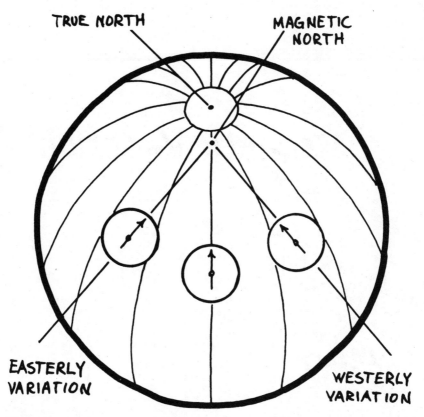

Fig. 18-2. *Magnetic variation is the angular difference between the magnetic north and true north.*

19

Magnetic Variation

Examine the map and find a location near one of the lines that show the magnetic variation. If the location is near the Mississippi River, the magnetic variation is 0 degrees (Fig. 19-1). The compass is pointing about true north. But if the location is near San Diego, the magnetic variation is about 15 degrees east (Fig. 19-2). Near Maine, it is about 20 degrees west (Fig. 19-3). To get a true heading, this angle is added to the compass heading. To convert a true heading into a compass heading, subtract the variation. For example, if you were in San Diego with a compass, and you wanted to go due east, or 90 degrees, you would go on a magnetic heading of 75 degrees. When you subtract 15 degrees (the easterly variation) from the true heading, 90 degrees, you get 75 degrees, the compass heading (Fig. 19-4).

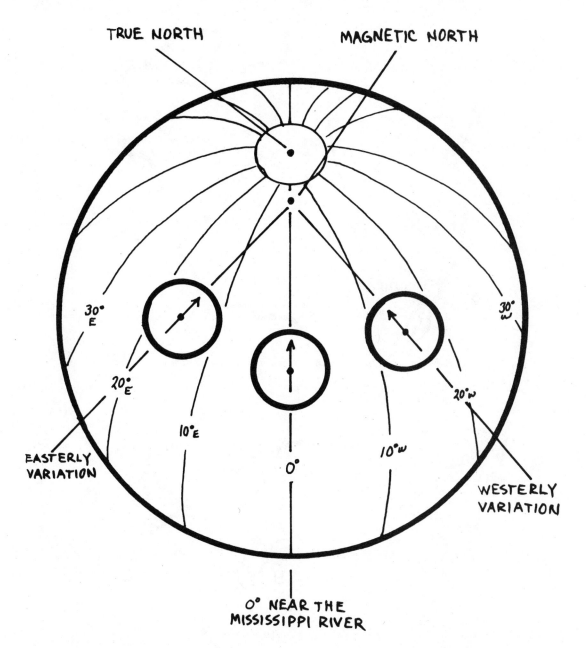

Fig. 19-1. *Near the Mississippi River a magnetic compass points about true north.*

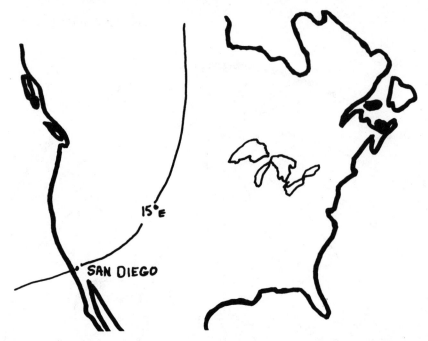

Fig. 19-2. *Near San Diego the magnetic variation is about 15 degrees east.*

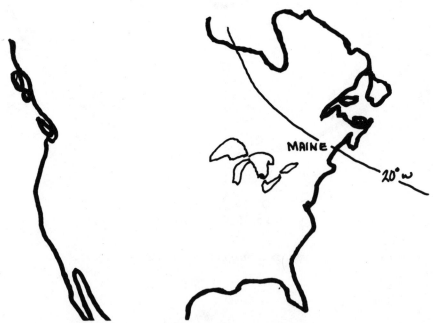

Fig. 19-3. *Near Maine the magnetic variation is about 20 degrees west.*

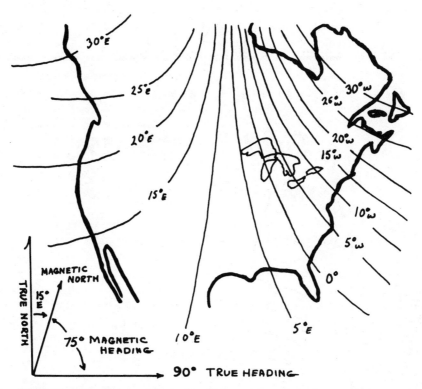

Fig. 19-4. *To convert a true heading into a magnetic heading subtract easterly variation and add westerly variation.*

20
Grid Patterns

Imagine a 25-acre pasture that contains horses. Draw a square to represent the pasture and make a dot to represent each horse (Fig. 20-1). You might want to use a scale in which 1 square inch represents 1 acre. You might have 100 horses—100 horses for 25 acres. You notice that some areas have more horses, others have fewer. To show which areas have the most horses, draw a grid made of 1-acre squares, and count the horses in each square (Fig. 20-2). This will express the densities of horses per acre (Fig. 20-3).

A simpler way to show density is to make a legend and use shading patterns to represent numbers (Fig. 20-4). Replace the numbers on the map with a shaded pattern that corresponds to that number. This shows at a glance the relationship between areas and quantities. Dot maps are more accurate, but by using a legend to show different categories, we've lost some accuracy in exchange for conveniency.

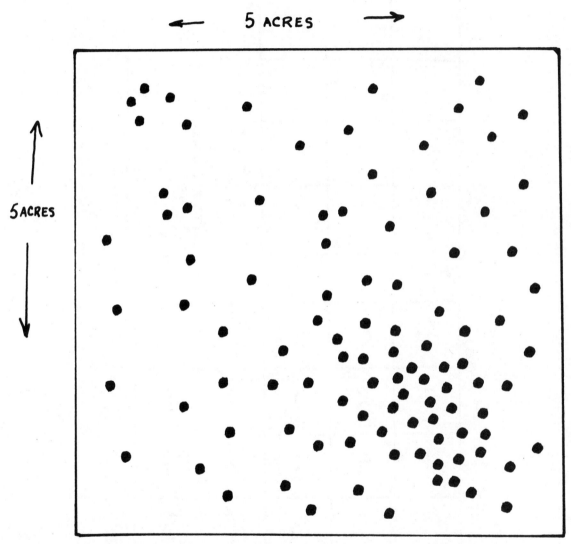

Fig. 20-1. *Make a dot to represent each horse in the pasture.*

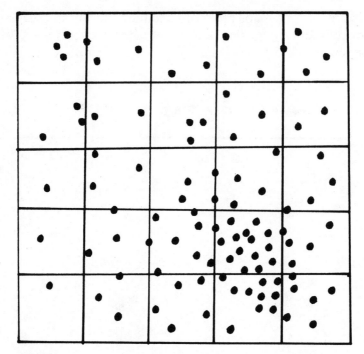

Fig. 20-2. *Count the horses in each square in the grid.*

4	2	2	3	3
3	2	3	3	2
1	4	2	6	4
1	3	8	15	5
1	2	5	10	6

Fig. 20-3. *The grid represents the densities of horses per acre.*

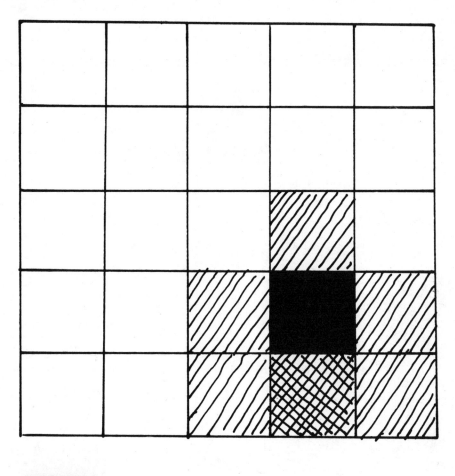

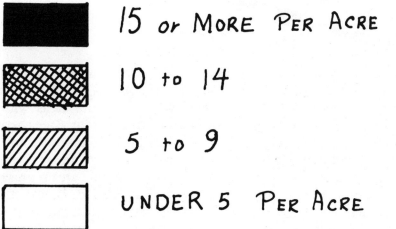

Fig. 20-4. *Shaded patterns can represent numbers of different densities.*

21

Isolines

Materials

- PENCIL
- PAPER
- NUMBERED GRID
  MAP FROM
  PREVIOUS
  ACTIVITY

Another way to show density is to find an area of a particular density, for example, 5 to 9 horses per square acre. Notice the other areas with the same density. When you join areas with a smooth line, you create an *isoline* from the ancient Greek word *iso*, meaning equal (Fig. 21-1). Find other areas of another density (10−14) and connect that area by a line. Connect the area with a density of 15 or more horses, and let the remaining area represent the under-5 density (Fig. 21-2). You have created an isoline map. This still might be confusing to read. Use a color or shaded pattern for each category (Fig. 21-3). Dark colors, or shades, tend to represent more density, whereas lighter shades represent less density. With the shaded areas, it should be easier to see the pattern of densities for a particular area.

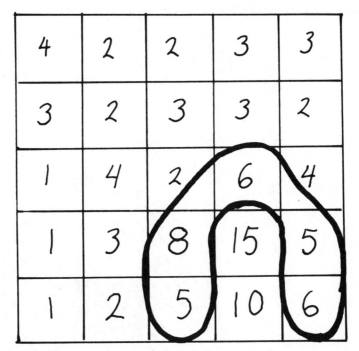

4	2	2	3	3
3	2	3	3	2
1	4	2	6	4
1	3	8	15	5
1	2	5	10	6

Fig. 21-1. *An isoline represents areas with the same density.*

4	2	2	3	3
3	2	3	3	2
1	4	2	6	4
1	3	8	15	5
1	2	5	10	6

Fig. 21-2. *The unshaded area represents a density of 5 or less.*

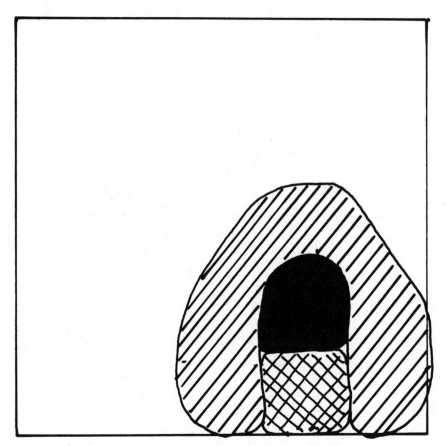

Fig. 21-3. Shaded patterns represent areas of similar densities.

22
Political Regions

Examine the map of North America shown in Fig. 22-1. You can see only a continent. Figure 22-2 shows the dotted lines of the boundaries between Canada, the United States, and Mexico. Place the paper over the map and trace the outline of North America. Include the dotted lines for the boundaries. Dotted lines help, but the map can be made easier to read. Shade, or color, the area inside each boundary. By using different colors, or shading, the different political regions become clearer (Fig. 22-3).

Maps that show the political regions are common. They provide a useful guide to help us see and understand the unfamiliar world that we live in.

Fig. 22-1. *Map of North America.*

Fig. 22-2. *Dotted lines represent boundaries.*

Fig. 22-3. *Shaded patterns represent different political regions.*

23
Middle, Average, Median, and Mean

Materials

- WORLD MAP OR GLOBE
- CITY MAP
- TRACING PAPER
- PENCIL
- RULER

Examine the map of the world, and notice the different surface area. The earth has a surface area of about 197 million square miles—that alone would be a lot to study. Geographers are interested in what takes place above the surface, as well as below. They also study people and what they do. To describe any of the information in a simple form, geographers let one thing represent many things. They use terms such as average, mean, middle, and median. Imagine four students who are taking a test. Three are not familiar with the subject, but one is. One student receives a grade of 30, two receive grades of 35, and one receives 100. To find the average, add the total scores and divide by the number of students (4). You find an average grade of 50. This is not a fair representation of the students, because one student brought the average well above the rest of the students. With few numbers, you receive unpredictable results. Use the largest population possible to find the average.

Examine the map of the city (Fig. 23-1). Draw a grid like the one in Fig. 23-2, and place it over the map. Notice the number of buildings inside each square. You can see that some areas have little or no buildings, whereas others have more (Fig. 23-3). Count the number of buildings in each square (Fig. 23-4). Add the numbers together to find the total number of buildings that are inside the grid. Assume that you counted 150. Divide the total by the number of squares in the grid (150 divided by 25). This is the density of a single representative square that reflects a larger number of squares. Here, there are an average of 6 buildings for each square mile.

Fig. 23-1. *A city map that shows buildings.*

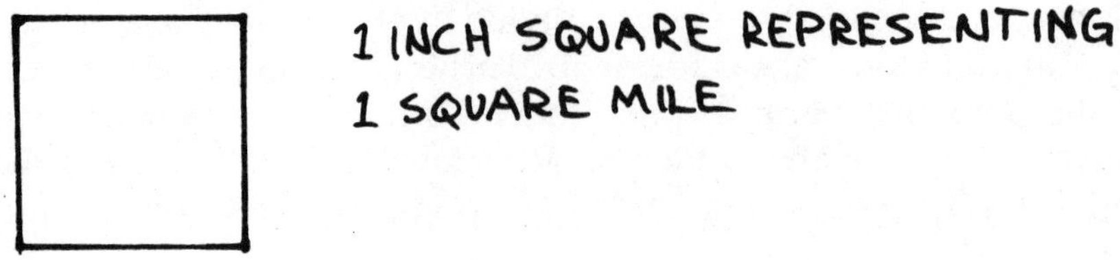

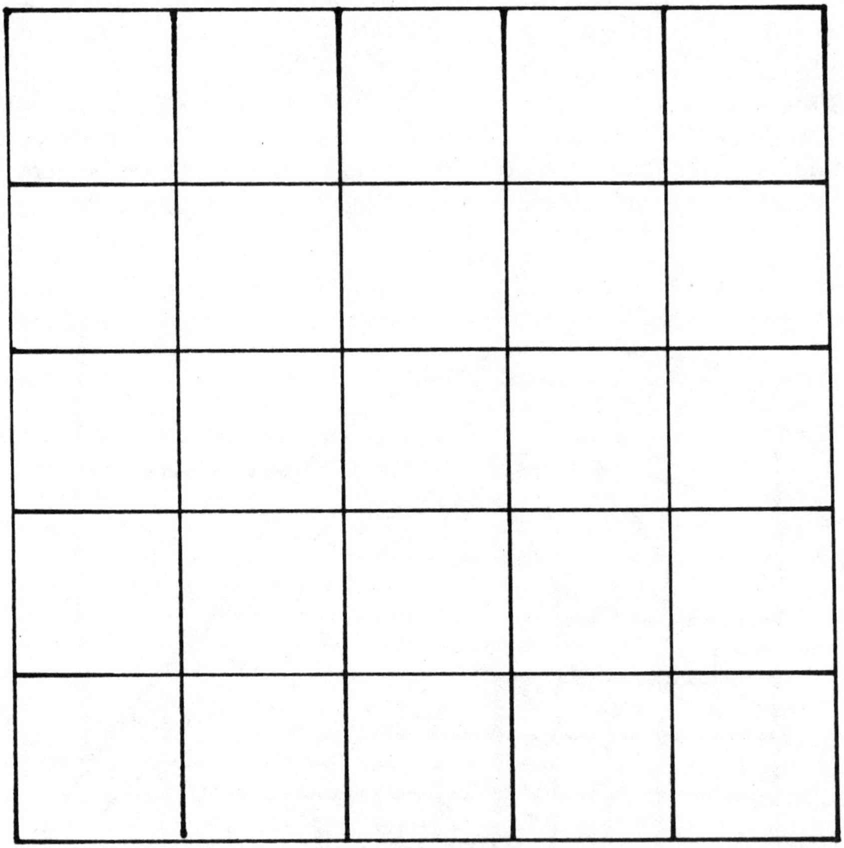

Fig. 23-2. *A grid that represents square miles.*

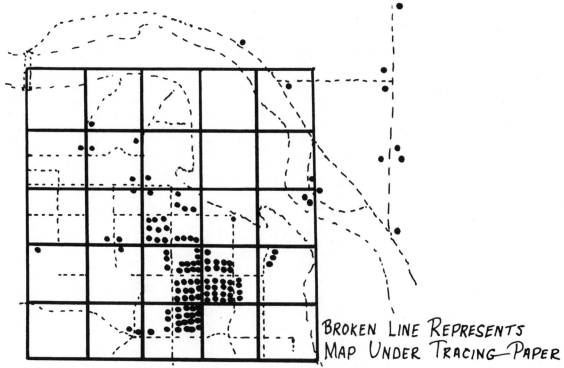

BROKEN LINE REPRESENTS
MAP UNDER TRACING PAPER

Fig. 23-3. *Some areas have few buildings, whereas other areas have many.*

Fig. 23-4. *Figures representing the number of buildings in each square mile.*

0	1	0	0	1
1	3	1	0	1
0	3	18	0	2
1	1	25	29	3
0	2	20	0	0

PART II

CHEMISTRY

1

An Experiment in Volume

Materials

- TABLE SALT
- WATER
- CLEAR DRINKING GLASS
- TRANSPARENT TAPE
- PENCIL
- TABLESPOON

Place a small piece of tape on the side of the glass about half way up. Make a line on the tape for a reference mark (Fig. 1-1), then fill the glass with water up to the line. Try to be precise in your measurements. Next, add one heaping tablespoon of salt to the water (Fig. 1-2). The water level will rise about one-eighth of an inch (Fig. 1-3). Mark this level on the tape. Now stir the water and salt until the salt is dissolved (Fig. 1-4). This can take a few minutes. Let the water stand and notice the level. It will be back to very near the reference mark.

Salt is made up of tiny crystals. The molecules in these crystals merge with the molecules of water to form a salty solution without increasing the volume of water.

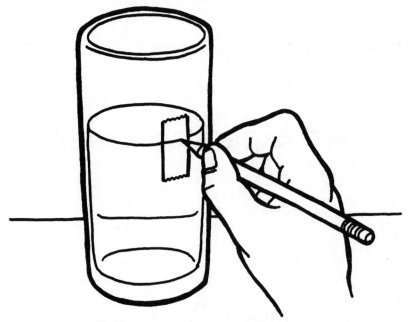

Fig. 1-1. Mark the level on the glass.

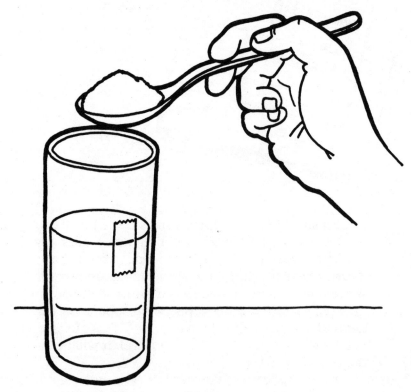

Fig. 1-2. Add salt to the water.

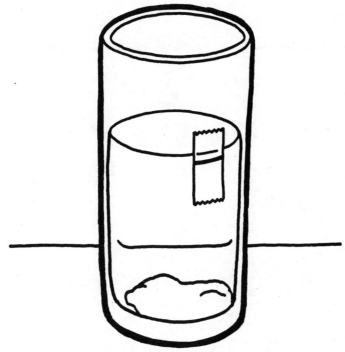

Fig. 1-3. *Notice that the water level has risen.*

Fig. 1-4. *The water level lowers as the salt dissolves.*

2

The Size of Water and Alcohol Molecules

Materials

- 2 JARS (ONE SMALL AND ONE TWICE AS LARGE)
- TRANSPARENT TAPE
- PENCIL
- RUBBING ALCOHOL
- WATER

Pour some water into the small jar and use the tape and pencil to mark the level of the water (Fig. 2-1). Pour this water into the larger jar (Fig. 2-2). Now fill the small jar to the same mark with water again and pour this in with the water into the larger jar. Mark the level in the larger jar (Fig. 2-3). Try to be accurate when you make the marks. Now, empty the large jar. Fill the small jar to the mark with rubbing alcohol and pour it into the large jar (Fig. 2-4). Then fill the small jar to the mark with water, and pour it in with the alcohol in the large jar (Fig. 2-5).

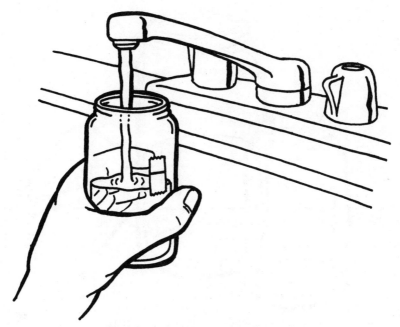

Fig. 2-1. *Fill the jar to the mark.*

Fig. 2-2. *Pour the measured amounts into the larger jar.*

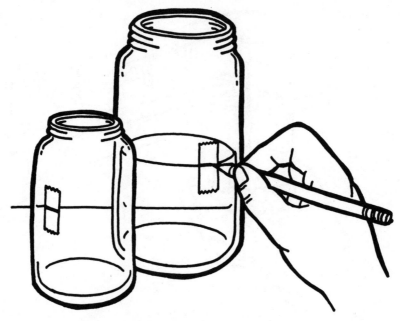

Fig. 2-3. Mark the level on the large jar.

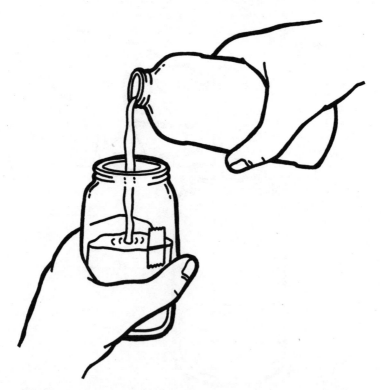

Fig. 2-4. Substitute alcohol for one of the measurements.

Fig. 2-5. *When water is mixed with alcohol, the level is lower.*

Notice that the level in the large jar is slightly below the mark. This shows that the water and alcohol takes up less space than water. The difference will not be much because of the small volumes used, but if one gallon of alcohol is mixed with one gallon of water, the result is about 3.5 percent less than two gallons.

This is because the molecules of alcohol fit into the spaces between molecules of water, much like pouring a volume of sand into an equal volume of gravel in a container. The sand fits into the spaces between the pieces of gravel.

3

Salt and the Melting Point of Ice

Materials

- 2 GLASSES
- 2 THERMOMETERS
- SALT
- ICE
- WATER
- TABLESPOON

Place a thermometer in each glass (Fig. 3-1) and fill both glasses with ice. Add a little water to each glass (Fig. 3-2). Watch the thermometers until both read 32 degrees. At this point, pour one tablespoon of salt into one of the glasses (Fig. 3-3) and notice the temperature of that thermometer. It should drop some.

As long as ice is melting in water, the temperature of the water will stay the same. But when salt is added, the freezing point of ice is lowered to below 32 degrees. This is how the ice in a home ice cream maker is brought to a low enough temperature to freeze the ice cream. Salt is added to the ice.

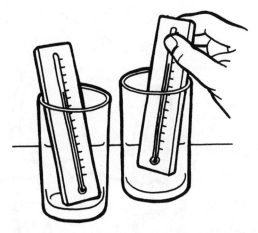

Fig. 3-1. *Put a thermometer in each glass.*

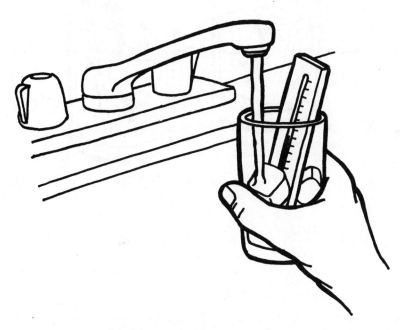

Fig. 3-2. *Add ice and water.*

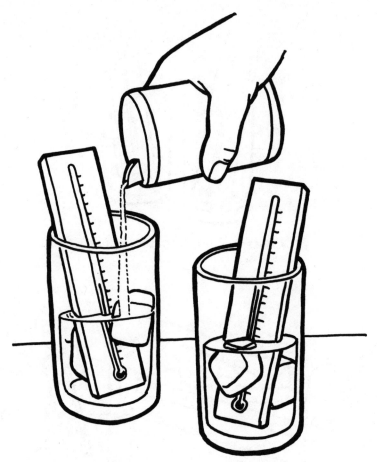

Fig. 3-3. *Salt lowers the freezing point of ice.*

4

How to Remove Iodine From Water

Materials

- MINERAL OIL (NOT VEG-ETABLE OIL) FROM A GROCERY OR DRUGSTORE
- IODINE
- MEDICINE DROPPER
- WATER
- SMALL JAR WITH LID
- TABLESPOON

Fill the jar about half full of water and add a few drops of iodine (Fig. 4-1). Replace the lid and shake the jar to mix the solution (Fig. 4-2). It should be light brown in color. Next, remove the lid and add a couple of tablespoons of mineral oil (Fig. 4-3). Replace the lid and shake the jar vigorously. Let the jar stand for a few minutes.

The solution will start to clear as the iodine separates from the water and is absorbed by the oil (Fig. 4-4). Most substances have a tendency to be more soluble, able to be dissolved, in some liquids more than in others. In this experiment, you found that iodine is more soluble in mineral oil than in water.

Fig. 4-1. *Add a few drops of iodine to the water.*

Fig. 4-2. *Shake the jar to mix the solution.*

Fig. 4-3. *Add a couple of tablespoons of mineral oil.*

Fig. 4-4. *The iodine is absorbed by the oil.*

5

How to Make a Salt

Over the sink or over some paper towels, fill the tablespoon about half full of vinegar (Fig. 5-1). Now sprinkle the baking soda over the vinegar (Fig. 5-2). Add baking soda until the bubbling stops. The mixture has now become a salt.

The bubbles were formed by carbon dioxide gas. The vinegar was an acid and the soda was a base (a supporting ingredient). When you add a soluble base (able to be dissolved) to an acid you will get a salt.

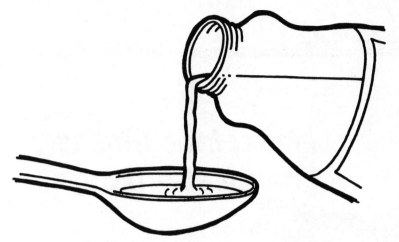

Fig. 5-1. *Pour a little vinegar into a spoon.*

Fig. 5-2. *Add sprinkles of baking soda.*

6

How Heat Makes Chemicals Change

Materials

- SUGAR
- OLD TEASPOON
- CANDLE AND MATCHES
- TIN PIE PLATE
- PROTECTIVE GLOVES OR POT HOLDER

Put a small amount of sugar in the spoon. Spread it out with your finger so that it makes a thin layer (Fig. 6-1). This will cause the sugar to heat evenly and melt faster. Light the candle over the pie plate and hold it at an angle so that the hot wax drips into the pan. Wearing protective gloves or using a pot holder, hold the spoon over the candle and heat the sugar (Fig. 6-2). Soon, the sugar will start to turn into a clear liquid. Keep the spoon in the flame and the sugar will turn brown and begin to bubble. Puffs of smoke will bubble up and the liquid will turn black and char, or scorch (Fig. 6-3). Remove the spoon from the flame. Be sure to set the spoon on a surface that will not melt or scorch.

Fig. 6-1. *Put a thin layer of sugar into a spoon.*

Fig. 6-2. *Heat the sugar until it turns black.*

Fig. 6-3. *Heat changed the sugar into carbon.*

Sugar is made up of carbon, hydrogen, and oxygen. The heat from the flame changed the hydrogen and oxygen into a vapor that was bubbled away into the air. And the carbon remained in the spoon in the form of a charred, lumpy mass.

7
Temperature's Effect on
Solids and Gases

Materials

- GLASS
- TABLESPOON
- SUGAR OR SALT
- COLD WATER
- WARM WATER
- COLD COLA
- WARM COLA
- KITCHEN CLOCK

Fill the glass about half full of cold water (Fig. 7-1). Add a tablespoon of sugar or salt, and stir the solution until the sugar or salt has dissolved. Notice how long it takes. Now, dump out the solution and rinse out the glass. Fill it about half full of warm water and stir in a tablespoon of sugar or salt (Fig. 7-2). Notice how long it takes for the sugar to dissolve this time. Dump the solution down the drain and rinse out the glass. Next, fill the glass about half full of cold cola (Fig. 7-3). Notice how it bubbles. Let the cola stand until it warms and becomes flat. Very few bubbles can be seen now.

The sugar dissolved much quicker in the warm water than the cold. Solutions made up of mostly water can hold more solids, such as sugar or salt, if the water is warm. If it were gases instead of

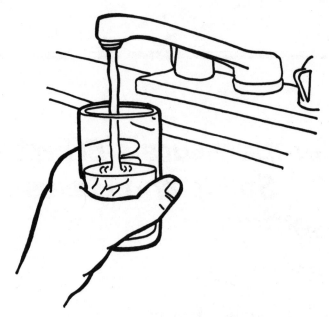

Fig. 7-1. Fill the glass with cold water.

Fig. 7-2. Sugar dissolves easier in warm water.

Fig. 7-3. *Bubbles of gas leave the cola as it warms.*

solids, however, the opposite would be true. The solution could hold more gases if it were cold.

When the sugar or salt, a solid, dissolved in the water, it became a liquid, absorbed heat, and lowered the temperature of the solution. So if the solution was heated, the solid would dissolve easier and faster. But the gas molecules in the cola solution began to move faster as the cola warmed and were forced to leave the solution. Heating a solid turns it into a liquid. Heating a liquid turns it into a gas.

8

Expanding Gas

Materials

- EMPTY 2-LITER POP BOTTLE
- COIN FOR BOTTLE OPENING (QUARTER)
- CUP OF WATER
- REFRIGERATOR

Put the bottle, without the lid, in the freezing compartment of the refrigerator for about 10 minutes (Fig. 8-1). After 10 minutes, wet the coin in the cup of water and remove the bottle from the freezer. Quickly place the wet coin over the mouth of the bottle (Fig. 8-2). The coin should be placed so that it forms a slight seal over the opening. In a few seconds, one edge of the coin will rise and fall (Fig. 8-3). This will continue until the air inside the bottle warms to the same temperature as the air in the room, or the coin moves out of position.

When the bottle was placed in the freezer, the air inside the bottle cooled. The air molecules contracted and took up less space. More cool air entered the bottle. When the bottle was placed in the

Fig. 8-1. *Place the bottle in the refrigerator.*

Fig. 8-2. *Place the wet coin over the opening.*

Fig. 8-3. *Expanding air causes the coin to lift.*

warmer air of the room, the cold air in the bottle began to warm and expand, taking up more space. As this air escaped from the bottle, it had enough pressure to lift the coin. When the pressure was released, the coin fell back down until the pressure inside built back up again. Cooling causes most things to contract. Heating causes expansion.

9

Testing for Starch

Materials

- IODINE
- WATER
- SMALL JAR
- PAPER TOWEL OR NEWSPAPER
- FOODS TO TEST (POTATO, APPLE, FLOUR, SALT, ETC.)
- KNIFE
- MEDICINE DROPPER

Place the paper towel or newspaper on a table or counter and put small amounts of each type of food on the paper (Fig. 9-1). Use the knife to cut slices from the potato and apple. Be very careful, and always hold the knife away from yourself. Never cut against your body. Pour a little water in the jar and add an equal amount of iodine (Figs. 9-2 and 9-3). Stir the solution. Now, using the medicine dropper, put a drop of the iodine solution on each food sample (Fig. 9-4). Drop the iodine on the cut part of the potato and apple.

Fig. 9-1. *Gather foods to test.*

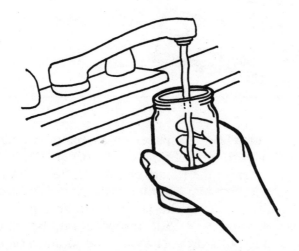

Fig. 9-2. *Pour water into the jar.*

Fig. 9-3. *Add an equal amount of iodine.*

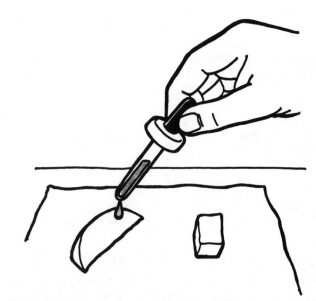

Fig. 9-4. *Test each food sample with the iodine solution.*

If the iodine turns dark brown or bluish purple, it means the food contains starch. What do the foods with starch have in common? You might have noticed that only the foods that come from plants contain starch. Throw the tested foods away when you have finished.

10

Testing for Starch in Toast

Materials

- GLASS
- DISH
- WATER
- IODINE
- SLICE OF WHITE BREAD
- TOASTER
- TEASPOON
- BUTTER KNIFE

Fill the glass about half full of water (Fig. 10-1). Add a teaspoon of iodine to the water (Fig. 10-2). Stir the solution then pour some into the dish (Fig. 10-3). Toast the bread. Now, carefully cut off a small section from the toast so that the edge is exposed to the white, untoasted center. Dip this edge into the iodine solution in the dish (Fig. 10-4). The white center of the toast will turn bluish purple, indicating the presence of starch. The toasted part should not change color.

The heat from the toaster changed the starch into dextrin. The chemical makeup of dextrin is very much like that of starch. Both are carbohydrates but dextrin is easier to digest. Dextrin causes the slightly sweet taste to the crust of bread. In our bodies, dextrin forms during digestion by the action of saliva and other body fluids on starch. This is why toast is easier to digest than plain bread. Discard the food after you have finished your test.

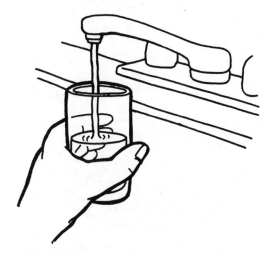

Fig. 10-1. Pour water into the glass.

Fig. 10-2. Add a teaspoon of iodine.

Fig. 10-3. *Pour the mixture into a dish.*

Fig. 10-4. *Dip a section of the toast into the solution.*

11

Testing Paper for Starch

Materials

- DIFFERENT TYPES OF PAPER (NEWSPAPER, WRITING PAPER, NOTE PAPER)
- SMALL GLASS
- IODINE
- WATER
- TABLE SPOON

Put two or three tablespoons of water in the glass and add an equal amount of iodine (Fig. 11-1). Stir the solution. Dip a strip of the paper to be tested into the iodine solution (Fig. 11-2). On some of the paper, the solution will not change color, but on some of the other strips, the solution will turn bluish black or black. This indicates the presence of starch in the paper. When some papers are made, a film of a starch solution is put on it to give the paper a smooth surface and to hold the fibers together. Laundry starch works the same way on clothes. It forms a thin film that stiffens the fabric and gives it a smooth surface.

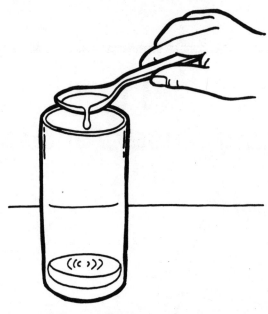

Fig. 11-1. *Put 2 or 3 tablespoons of water into the glass.*

Fig. 11-2. *Dip strips of paper into the solution to test for starch.*

12
Testing for Hard Water

Materials

- DISTILLED WATER (FROM GROCERY STORE)
- TAP WATER
- 3 JARS WITH LIDS
- MEDICINE DROPPER
- BAR OF SOAP
- FOOD GRATER
- TABLESPOON
- PENCIL, PAPER, AND TAPE

Grate a few soap flakes from the bar of soap (Fig. 12-1). Place one tablespoon of soap flakes into one of the jars, then add six tablespoons of hot water to the jar (Fig. 12-2). Mix the contents into a soapy solution and label the jar "soap."

Fill another jar about two-thirds full of tap water and label this jar "tap water." Pour the same amount of distilled water into the third jar. Place the jars side by side so that you will have equal amounts of tap water and distilled water. Label the last jar "distilled water" (Fig. 12-3).

Use the medicine dropper and add five drops of the soap solution to the jar of tap water (Fig. 12-4). Screw the lid on tight and shake the jar (Fig. 12-5). Does the soap lather? If it doesn't, add five

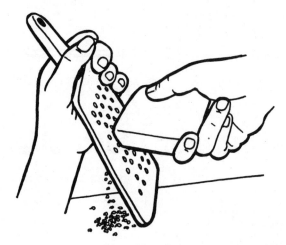

Fig. 12-1. *Grate a few flakes of soap from a bar.*

Fig. 12-2. *Add 6 tablespoons of hot water to the soap flakes.*

more drops of soap solution and shake it again. Continue adding drops of soap solution until it lathers. Count the drops to see how many it required to get it to lather.

Now, repeat the same test on the jar of distilled water. Count how many drops of soap solution it needed to get it to lather. Compare the numbers and see which type of water needed the most soap to make it lather.

The water that needed very little soap is said to be "soft water." Water that needs a lot of soap is called "hard water." In your test, the tap water should have needed more soap than the distilled water. This is because of the chemicals usually found in tap

Fig. 12-3. Label each jar.

Fig. 12-4. Add 5 drops of soap solution to the tap water.

water. The chemicals are calcium salts. The calcium in the salts reacts with the soap and makes a film. More soap must be added until all of the calcium in the water is used up, then the soap will lather. You might want to save the soap solution for other experiments.

Fig. 12-5. *Shake the jar to see if the soap lathers.*

13

How to Make Hard Water Soft

Materials

- SOAP SOLUTION (SEE EXPERIMENT 12)
- TAP WATER
- WASHING SODA (NEXT TO THE LAUNDRY DETERGENT IN GROCERY STORE)
- JAR
- MEASURING SPOONS
- MEDICINE DROPPER

Fill the jar with six tablespoons of tap water. Stir in one teaspoon of washing soda (Fig. 13-1). Continue to stir until the washing soda has dissolved. Now, add drops of soap solution and shake the jar (Figs. 13-2 and 13-3). Count the number of drops of soap solution it takes to get a lather. It should take much less soap to produce a lather than in the previous experiment. The washing soda has removed the hardness from the water.

Washing soda is made from sodium carbonate. The carbonate part of the soda combines with the calcium in the hard water and makes calcium carbonate. When this happens, the calcium is unable to react with the soap and the soap can lather.

Fig. 13-1. *Stir in a teaspoon of washing soda.*

Fig. 13-2. *Add drops of soap solution.*

Fig. 13-3. *Shake the jar to see if the soap lathers.*

14

How Stalactites and Stalagmites Form

Materials

- 2 JARS
- HEAVY COTTON STRING
- CARDBOARD
- EPSOM SALTS (FROM GROCERY STORE)
- WATER
- TABLESPOON

Fill each jar about two-thirds full of water. Stir in several tablespoons of Epsom salts to each jar of water (Fig. 14-1). Keep adding salt until you have a thick solution. Now, place the jars a few inches apart on the cardboard. Lower one end of the string into one of the jars and the other end of the string into the other jar (Fig. 14-2). Let the part of the string between the jars sag to form a shallow "v."

After a few days, you will find an icicle formation growing down from the string and another growing up from the cardboard (Fig. 14-3). The one growing down is called a stalactite, and the one growing up is called a stalagmite.

Fig. 14-1. *Stir in several tablespoons of Epsom salts.*

Fig. 14-2. *Lower a string into the jars.*

Fig. 14-3. *After a few days stalactites and stalagmites will begin to form.*

In a cave, drops of water containing dissolved limestone, fall to the floor. Limestone is made of calcium carbonate and this dissolves in the water that flows over limestone rocks. Specks of calcium carbonate build up when the water evaporates. This continues year after year to make the formations.

In this experiment, the salt in the solution travels up the string and is deposited where the water drips. The salt remains after the water evaporates, creating the stalactites and stalagmites.

15

How to Make Bath Salts

Materials

- SODIUM CARBONATE
- COLOGNE OR PERFUME
- PLASTIC BAG
- ROLLING PIN OR JAR
- FOOD COLORING
- JAR WITH LID
- TABLESPOON
- 2 OR 3 PAPER TOWELS
- BOWL

You can buy sodium carbonate, or washing soda, from the grocery store. Put about five tablespoons of washing soda into the plastic bag (Fig. 15-1). Don't use the white, powdery lumps usually found near the top of the box. Use the clear crystals just under these. Place the paper towels, one on top of the other, on a table or counter. The towels will make a softer surface for breaking up the crystals. Put the bag of washing soda on the towels and use the rolling pin to break the crystals into smaller pieces (Fig. 15-2).

Next, empty the broken crystals into the bowl (Fig. 15-3). Add about five drops of cologne or perfume and about five drops of food coloring to the crystals (Fig. 15-4). Stir the crystals until they

Fig. 15-1. *Put about 5 tablespoons of washing soda into a plastic bag.*

Fig. 15-2. *Break the crystals into smaller pieces.*

Fig. 15-3. *Pour the broken crystals into a bowl.*

Fig. 15-4. *Add drops of cologne and food coloring to the crystals.*

are all brightly colored. Pour the crystals into the jar and put on the lid. Label the jar "bath salts" and keep the lid in place until you're ready to use your bath salts (Fig. 15-5).

Bath salts make hard bath water soft and the soap easier to lather. They also keep the soap from making a film.

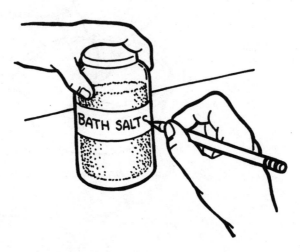

Fig. 15-5. Label the jar.

16

How Soap Works

Materials

- JAR WITH LID
- SMALL PIECE OF RAG
- POWDERED LAUNDRY DETERGENT
- COOKING GREASE OR SHORTENING
- WATER

Fill the jar about half full of water, then add some laundry detergent and mix into a soapy solution (Fig. 16-1). Smear a small glob of grease on the rag and drop the rag into the soapy solution (Figs. 16-2 and 16-3). Replace the lid and shake the jar for a couple of minutes. Remove the rag and most, if not all, of the grease will be gone from the rag (Fig. 16-4).

Soap molecules are long. One end will dissolve in water and the other will dissolve in oil. One end of the molecule works on the particles of grease and the other end stays in the molecules of water. As more and more ends of the soap molecules try to work into the grease, they come between the grease and the cloth. They continue

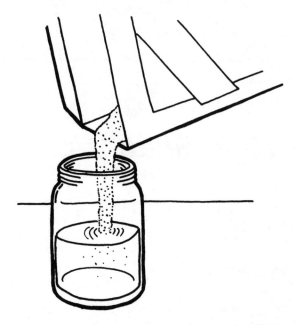

Fig. 16-1. *Add washing powder to the water.*

Fig. 16-2. *Smear grease on a rag.*

Fig. 16-3. *Put the rag into the solution and shake the jar.*

Fig. 16-4. *Most of the grease should be gone.*

to force the grease from the rag and break it up into tiny balls. Each of these tiny balls is covered with a water-liking film. This film keeps the tiny balls of grease from combining and they remain in the water when the rag is removed.

17
Soap that Eats an Egg

Materials

- 2 JARS
- EGG (HARD-BOILED)
- POWDERED LAUNDRY DETERGENT (SOME WITH ENZYMES, SOME WITHOUT)
- TABLESPOON AND KNIFE
- WARM WATER
- PAPER, PEN, AND TAPE

Put a tablespoon of the laundry detergent containing enzymes in one of the jars and label it "enzyme." Put a tablespoon of the other laundry detergent in the other jar and label it "regular." Now put eight tablespoons of warm water in each jar (Fig. 17-1).

Have an adult help you boil an egg. When the egg is completely cooled and peeled, carefully cut two pieces of the egg white exactly the same size (Fig. 17-2) and put one piece in each jar.

Place both jars in a warm location, such as near a vent, and let them set for two days (Fig. 17-3). After two days, remove both pieces of egg white from the jars and compare their size. The one from the jar labeled enzyme should be smaller.

Fig. 17-1. *Put 8 tablespoons of warm water into each jar.*

Fig. 17-2. *Cut 2 pieces of egg white the same size.*

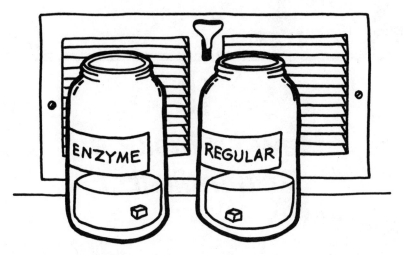

Fig. 17-3. *Place the jars in a warm place for two days.*

Enzyme is a protein-like substance formed in plant and animal cells. The enzyme attacks the particles in the egg white and breaks them into smaller particles. These smaller particles then dissolve in the water. The piece of egg from the other jar should have remained the same size. This shows that the egg did not dissolve in regular laundry detergent.

Did you know we have enzymes in our stomachs? They break the food particles into small molecules that can dissolve into our blood.

18

How to Make an Acid Indicator

Materials

- RED CABBAGE
- TEAKETTLE AND PAN
- LARGE SPOON AND KNIFE
- PAPER TOWEL
- FUNNEL
- BOTTLE WITH A LID
- WATER
- STOVE
- POT HOLDERS
- CUTTING BOARD

Have an adult help you pour some water in the teakettle and heat it on the stove. While the water is heating, carefully chop up about one-fourth of the cabbage (Fig. 18-1). Place the pieces of cabbage in the pan. When the water comes to a boil, pour some over the pieces of cabbage (Fig. 18-2), just enough to cover them. Be extremely careful—hot water can burn! Also, use pot holders because the handle will become hot. Stir the cabbage, then let the pieces soak for about 20 minutes.

Fig. 18-1. *Chop up part of a red cabbage.*

Fig. 18-2. *Cover the pieces with boiling water.*

Make a filter by folding the paper towel in half twice, then separate one of the corners to make a pocket. This shapes the paper towel into a cone. Place the funnel into the bottle and then put the cone into the funnel (Fig. 18-3). Pour the cabbage pieces and liquid into the funnel (Fig. 18-4). The paper towel filter will separate the purple-colored liquid from the cabbage. Screw on the lid and label the bottle "indicator" (Fig. 18-5). You can save this indicator solution for other experiments.

If you pour a small amount of indicator in a jar, then drop in a substance to be tested, the indicator will change color. If the indicator turns pink, the substance was an acid. If the indicator turned blue or green, the substance belonged to a group of chemicals known as alkalis. In some tests, it might take an hour or so for the indicator to change color.

Fig. 18-3. *Fold the paper towel into a filter.*

Fig. 18-4. *Pour the mixture through the filter.*

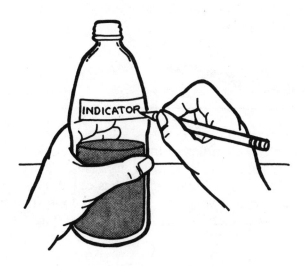

INDICATOR

Fig. 18-5. *Label the bottle.*

19

How to Make Paper Indicators

Materials

- PAPER TOWEL OR PAPER COFFEE FILTER
- LIQUID INDICATOR (SEE EXPERIMENT 18)
- BOWL
- BAKING PAN
- SCISSORS
- PLASTIC SANDWICH BAG

Pour about a cup of indicator into the bowl. Soak the paper in the bowl then place it on the pan to dry (Figs. 19-1 and 19-2). The paper should be light blue. After it has dried, cut the paper into strips about one inch wide and four inches long. The strips can be stored in the sandwich bag until ready to use (Fig. 19-3).

Fig. 19-1. *Soak the paper in the indicator.*

Fig. 19-2. *Place the paper in a pan to dry.*

Fig. 19-3. *Cut the paper into strips. Store the strips in a sandwich bag.*

PART III

METEOROLOGY

1

How Heat Is Transferred by Radiation

Materials

- electric lamp
- hand

Hold your hand, with the palm up, a few inches under the lamp and turn it on. Notice that you begin to feel the heat almost as soon as you turn on the lamp (Fig. 1-1). The heat is carried to your hand by very short waves of radiant energy. This form of energy can leave its source and travel through empty space at 186,000 miles a second. Radiant energy is not heat, but it can be changed into heat. When radiant energy strikes a material that can absorb it, it makes the molecules that make up the material move faster. This changes the radiant energy into heat energy. The sun warms the earth by radiant energy.

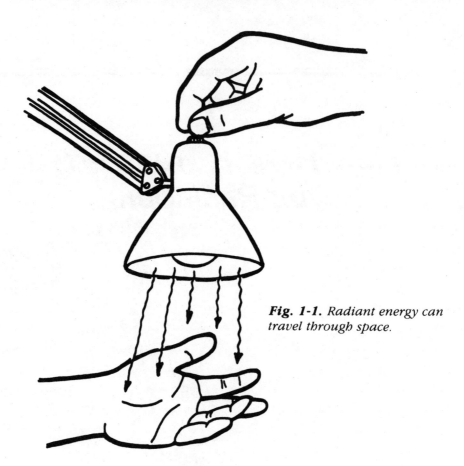

Fig. 1-1. Radiant energy can travel through space.

2

Materials that Absorb Radiant Energy

Materials

- 2 tin cans
- 2 thermometers
- soil
- water
- sunlight

Fill one can full of water and the other can full of soil (Figs. 2-1 and 2-2). Stand one thermometer in the water and insert the other into the soil (Fig. 2-3). Read the temperatures of the water and the soil. Now place both cans in sunlight and watch the readings on the thermometers (Fig. 2-4).

Notice that the temperature of the soil begins to rise first. This is because the soil absorbs heat faster than water. If the cans are removed from the sunlight and placed in the shade, the soil will also lose heat faster than the water. The wind along a beach blows in different directions from day to night. During the day, the warm earth heats the air above it. This warm air rises as the cooler air from the sea blows in. At night, the wind direction reverses. The earth loses heat and the warmer water heats the air above it. This air rises as the cooler air from the shore blows out to sea.

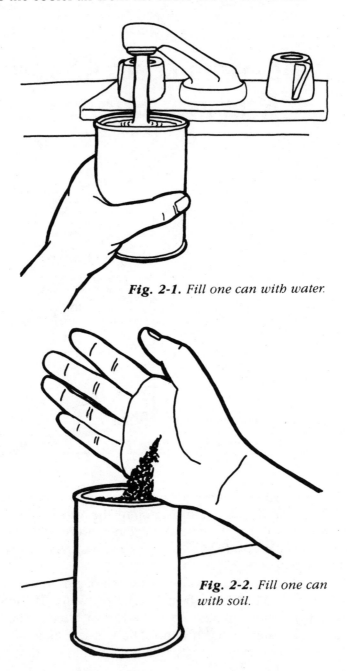

Fig. 2-1. Fill one can with water.

Fig. 2-2. Fill one can with soil.

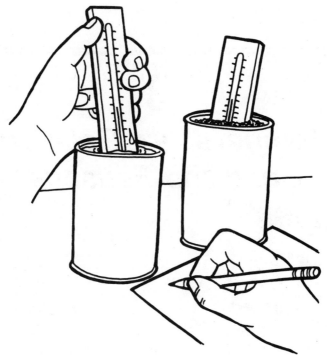

Fig. 2-3. *Place a thermometer in each can.*

Fig. 2-4. *The temperature of the soil begins to rise first.*

3

Temperature Patterns and the Seasons

Materials

• Flashlight
• Piece of paper

Turn the flashlight on and aim it straight down at the piece of paper. Notice that the light will be concentrated in a circle (Fig. 3-1). Now, hold the flashlight at an angle. The light will be weaker and spread out over a larger area (Fig. 3-2).

The angle that the sun's rays strike the earth is what determines the temperature. Sunshine strikes the earth near the equator from directly overhead, or at about 90 degrees. But near the polar regions, the rays come in more slanted, much less than 90 degrees. This is what causes the difference in the temperatures between the equator and the poles.

The changing angle of the sun's rays also causes the change in the seasons. In the summer, the sun's rays strike the earth at a high angle. The sun's energy is more concentrated and has less atmosphere to travel through. In the winter, the sun is lower in the sky. When the rays are spread over a larger area, they cannot heat the earth as much. The sun's rays must also travel through more of the earth's atmosphere. Much of the energy is absorbed in the atmosphere or scattered back into space, never reaching the earth.

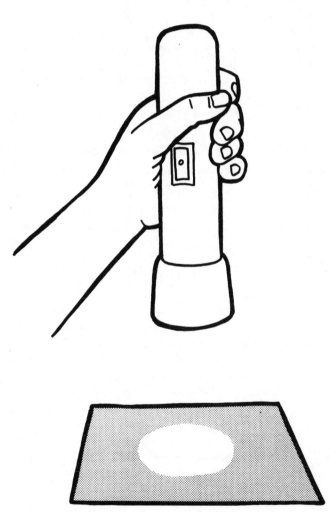

Fig. 3-1. *The light is concentrated in a small area.*

Fig. 3-2. *When the light strikes at an angle, it spreads over a larger area.*

4

The Coriolis Force

Materials

- globe
- chalk

Place one hand on top of the globe and slowly turn it in the same direction that the earth spins. This will be to the right, or counterclockwise looking down at the North Pole (Fig. 4-1). As the globe turns, draw a chalk line directly down from the North Pole toward the South Pole (Fig. 4-2). Now, stop the globe and examine the chalk line. It will not be a straight line but a curved one that crosses the equator at an angle. The chalk line will look as if it were drawn from the northeast toward the southwest.

The warm air near the equator is lighter than the cooler air near the poles. Because of this, there is a permanent low-pressure

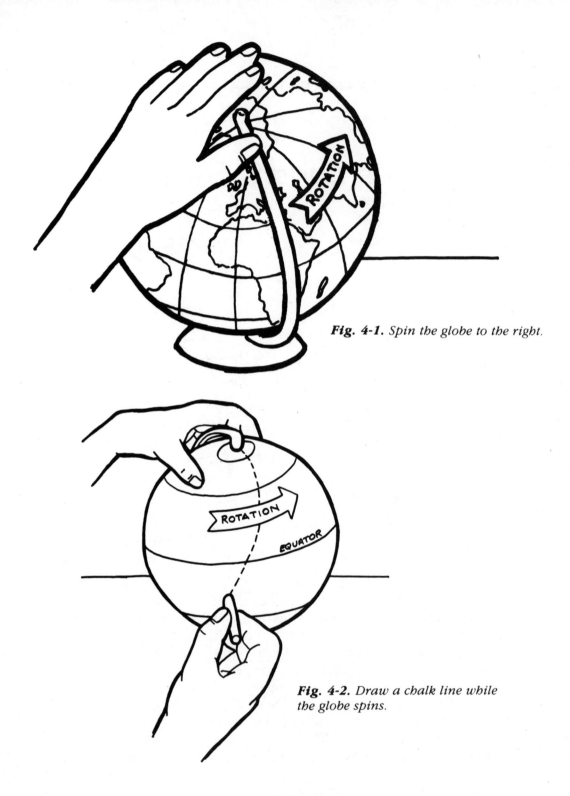

Fig. 4-1. *Spin the globe to the right.*

Fig. 4-2. *Draw a chalk line while the globe spins.*

area around the earth near the equator called the equatorial low. The cooler air at the poles sinks to the earth, forming areas of polar highs. This heavier air moves toward the equator forcing the warmer air upward into the upper atmosphere. This warm air in the upper atmosphere now moves toward the poles. Air moves from the poles to the equator and back to the poles in a continuous cycle (Fig. 4-3).

Air masses do not move directly north or south, however. The rotation of the earth creates a force called the Coriolis force. This force causes the air currents to curve to the right of the direction that they are traveling in the Northern Hemisphere and curve to the left of the direction they're moving in the Southern Hemisphere.

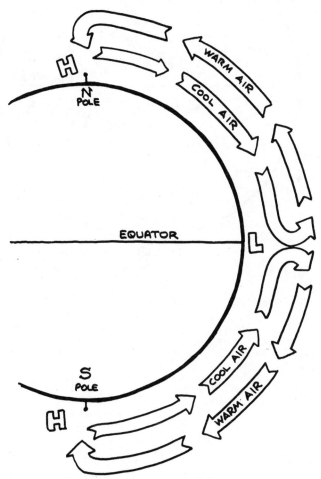

Fig. 4-3. *Air travels back and forth in a continuous cycle.*

This means that the winds blowing toward the equator to replace the rising air are from the northeast in the Northern Hemisphere and from the southeast in the Southern Hemisphere. These winds are called the trade winds (Fig. 4-4).

Over the equatorial regions, air moves constantly upward and is not felt as wind. Sailors call this region the belt of equatorial calms.

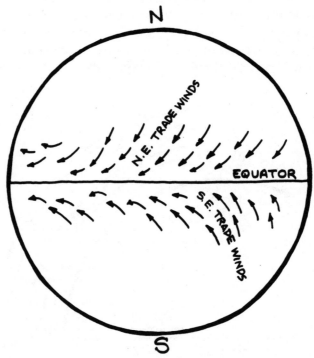

Fig. 4-4. *The rotation of the earth causes the trade winds.*

5

Why Warm Air Rises

Materials
- paper and pencil
- scissors
- metal thimble
- needle
- spool (sewing thread)
- wood pencil with eraser
- table lamp

Mark the pattern of a spiral on the paper (Fig. 5-1). Cut the pattern from the paper but leave enough space in the center to partially insert the thimble (Fig. 5-2). Make the turns about an inch wide. Make a hole in the center and press the bottom of the thimble part way through the hole (Fig. 5-3).

Next, insert the needle upside down into the eraser (Fig. 5-4). Remove the threaded nut from the top of the lamp shade and place the spool over the threaded stud (Fig. 5-5). Place the pointed end of the pencil into the hole in the spool. Carefully set the thimble in the spiral over the point of the needle (Fig. 5-6). The point of the

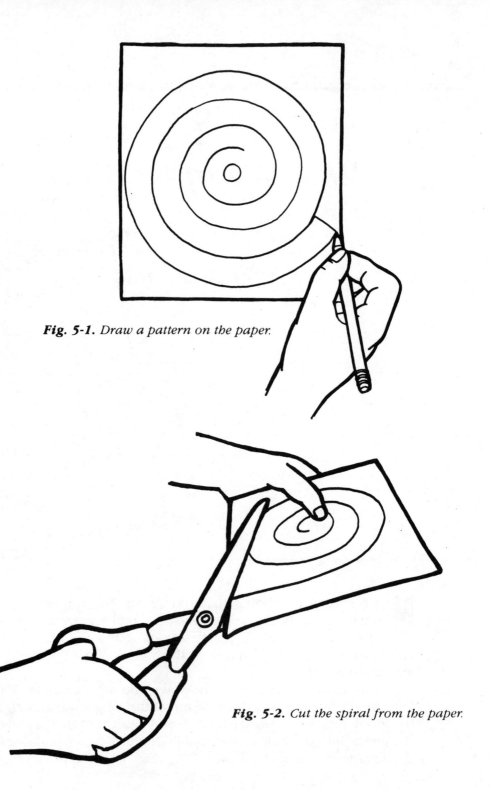

Fig. 5-1. *Draw a pattern on the paper.*

Fig. 5-2. *Cut the spiral from the paper.*

needle makes very little contact with the thimble and this makes a very good pivot point with little friction.

Turn on the lamp and, after a few minutes, the spiral will begin to turn. The lamp heats the air and the molecules of air expand, making the air lighter. Cooler, heavier air moves in and pushes the warm air up. The warm air pushes on the spiral and it begins to turn.

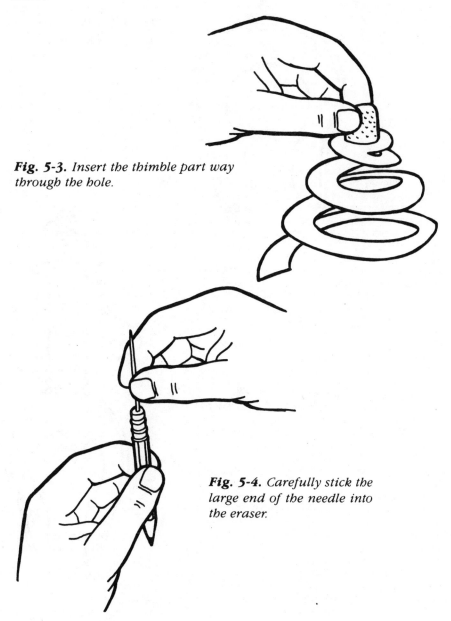

Fig. 5-3. *Insert the thimble part way through the hole.*

Fig. 5-4. *Carefully stick the large end of the needle into the eraser.*

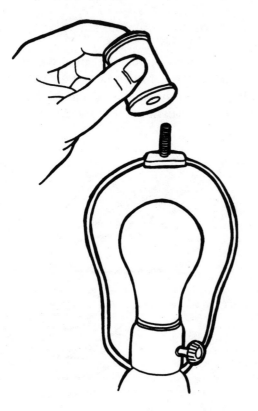

Fig. 5-5. *Place the spool over the threaded stud.*

Fig. 5-6. *Warm air rising will cause the spiral to turn.*

6
Convection Currents

Materials

- refrigerator

Open the refrigerator door a few inches, and place your hand near the opening at the top (Fig. 6-1). You should feel a warm draft blowing in the opening. Now place your hand at the opening near the bottom (Fig. 6-2). You will feel a cold draft coming out.

When air moves, it becomes wind, or a current of air. When the refrigerator door was opened, the cold, dense air inside quickly moved out into the warmer air in the room. The warmer air was lighter and was pushed up by the cooler air. Warm air from the room rushed into the top of the opening to fill the space left by the cold air. This air is cooled and continues the circulation pattern.

Gravity pulls the cold air down because cold air is dense and heavy. This air moves under the warm air and pushes it up, because warm air is less dense and this makes it lighter. Temperature affects the weather more than anything else.

Fig. 6-1. *Warm air is pulled into the top of the opening.*

Fig. 6-2. Gravity pulls the cold air down and out into the room.

7

The Weight of the Atmosphere

Materials

- gallon can with lid
- cup
- water
- stove
- protective gloves or pot holders
- sink

Pour one cup of water in the can (Fig. 7-1) and, leaving the lid off, place the can on the stove. Have an adult help you heat the water to a boil and, using the gloves, carefully remove the can from the stove (Fig. 7-2). Quickly replace the lid. Now, place the can in the sink and run cold water over the sides of the can (Fig. 7-3). It will instantly collapse because of the air pressure pushing on the outside of the can.

When you suck up lemonade through a straw, you might think that the suction is caused by a pull from the inside of the straw. But what really makes the lemonade go up the straw is a push from the

Fig. 7-1. *Pour the cup of water into the can.*

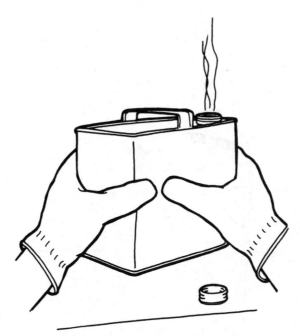

Fig. 7-2. *Use gloves to remove the can.*

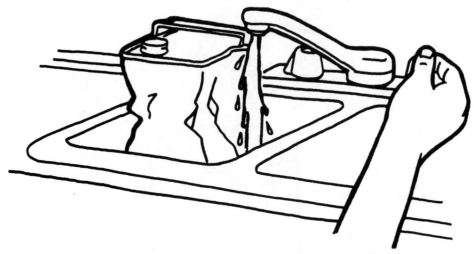

Fig. 7-3. *Atmospheric pressure causes the can to collapse.*

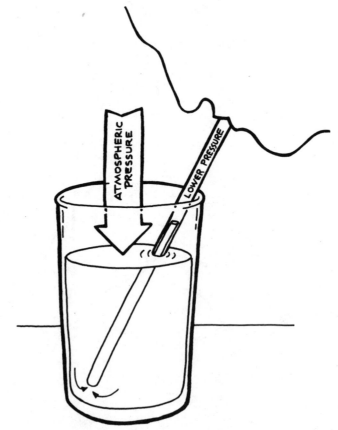

Fig. 7-4. *Atmospheric pressure forces the liquid up the straw.*

outside. Air is pulled down by gravity just like solids and liquids. This downward pull causes air to have pressure. Sucking on the straw lowered the pressure inside the straw and allowed atmospheric pressure to push the lemonade up into the straw (Fig. 7-4).

Our atmosphere surrounds the earth and is divided into four zones: the troposphere, the stratosphere, the ionosphere, and the exosphere. The troposphere is the air from the earth to about 10 miles up; the stratosphere is the air from 10 miles to 60 miles up; the ionosphere is from 60 to 120 miles up; and the exosphere includes all of the air beyond 120 miles above the earth (Fig. 7-5). Atmospheric pressure is measured in atmospheres. An atmosphere is a pressure of 14.7 pounds to the square inch of surface.

Simple lift pumps such as those found in a well use the atmospheric pressure to pump water. It works by removing the air inside the pipe so that the atmospheric pressure pushes water into it. The water comes up the pipe and flows out of a spout. The atmospheric pressure is only great enough to push water up about 34 feet. When the cylinder of a lift pump is more than about 34 feet above the water in a well, it can't pump any water.

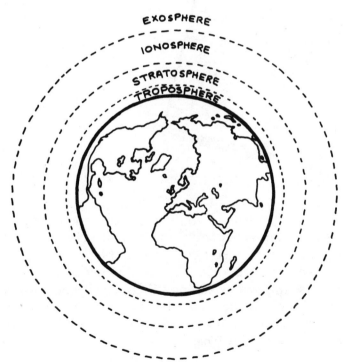

Fig. 7-5. *Our atmosphere is divided into zones.*

8

Compressed Air Is Heavier

Materials

- yardstick
- 2 balloons
- 3 strings (each about 18 inches long)

- paper clip
- pin or needle
- chair or rod

Tie one end of the strings around the exact center of the yardstick (Fig. 8-1). Tie the other end to the back of a chair or a rod so that the yardstick is suspended freely and can be balanced (Fig. 8-2).

Blow up both balloons to about the same size and tie off the openings. Use the two remaining strings to suspend a balloon from each end of the yardstick. One balloon will probably be heavier than the other, so attach the paper clip to the yardstick and move it along until the yardstick balances (Fig. 8-3).

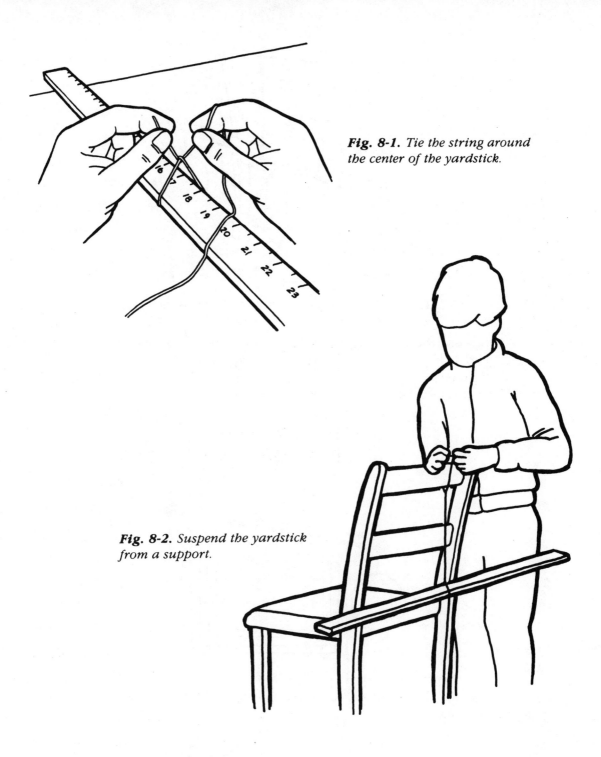

Fig. 8-1. Tie the string around the center of the yardstick.

Fig. 8-2. Suspend the yardstick from a support.

Fig. 8-3. *Move the paper clip to balance the balloons.*

Use the pin or needle to puncture one of the balloons. The yardstick is no longer balanced (Fig. 8-4). This means that compressed air (the air trapped in the balloon) has weight and weighs more than an equal volume of normal air.

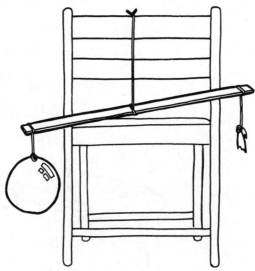

Fig. 8-4. *When one balloon was popped, the yardstick was no longer balanced.*

9

How to Pour Cold Air

Materials
- large jar with lid
- small piece of paper
- match
- refrigerator (freezer section)

Wad up the small piece of paper and carefully light it with the match. Blow out the paper (Fig. 9-1) and drop it in the jar. You want to capture the smoke, so quickly replace the lid (Fig. 9-2). Place the jar in the freezing compartment of the refrigerator (Fig. 9-3). After about 10 minutes, take the jar into a room where there are no drafts. Remove the lid. Very little of the smokey air will come out. Turn the jar upside down. The smoke will pour out and sink toward the floor (Fig. 9-4).

The cold air in the jar is more dense than the warmer air in the room. The more dense it is, the heavier it is. Therefore, when you opened the jar right side up, little of the smokey air was able to rise out of the jar. But when you turned the jar upside down, the denser, heavier air sank.

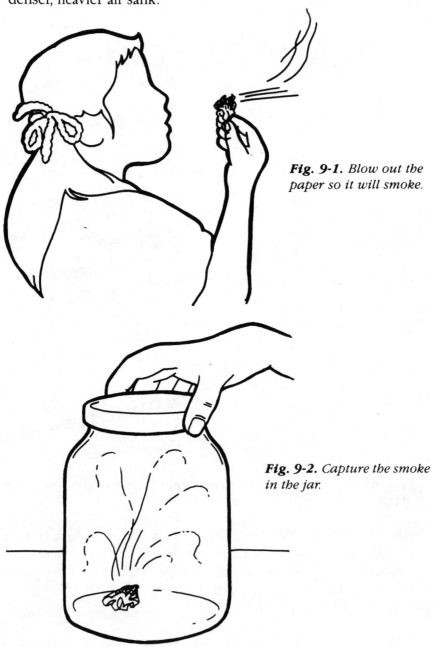

Fig. 9-1. *Blow out the paper so it will smoke.*

Fig. 9-2. *Capture the smoke in the jar.*

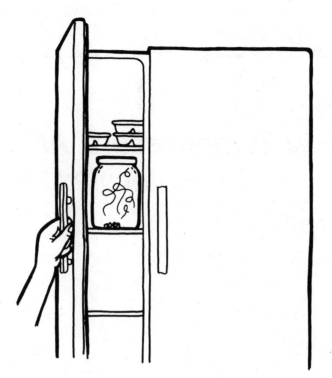

Fig. 9-3. *Cool the air inside the jar.*

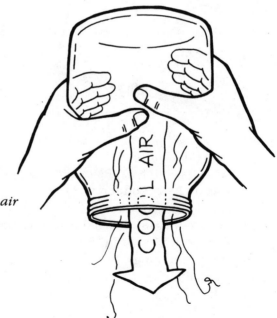

Fig. 9-4. *Pour the cold air from the jar.*

10

How Temperature Affects Air Molecules

Materials

- balloon
- tape measure
- refrigerator

Blow up the balloon and tie a knot in the opening (Fig. 10-1). You don't want it to leak. Place the tape measure around the balloon and measure its circumference (Fig. 10-2). Place the balloon in the refrigerator for about a half hour (Fig. 10-3). Remove the balloon and measure it again. It will be much smaller (Fig. 10-4).

When you blew up the balloon, you used the warm air from your mouth and lungs. When this air cooled, the molecules, or tiny particles making up the air, became smaller and more dense. This means that they took up less space and made the balloon smaller.

Fig. 10-1. *Blow up the balloon.*

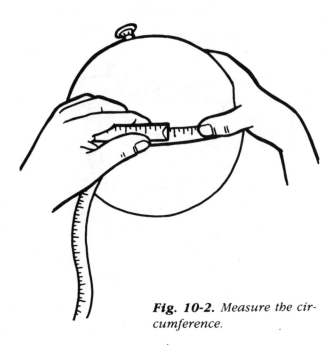

Fig. 10-2. *Measure the cir-cumference.*

Fig. 10-3. *Cool the air in the balloon.*

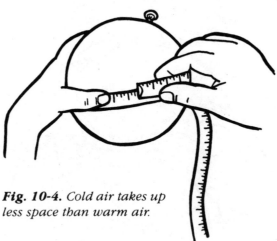

Fig. 10-4. *Cold air takes up less space than warm air.*

11

How Evaporation Cools

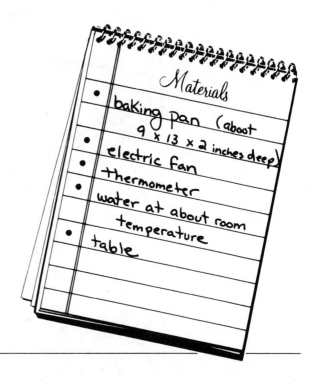

Materials

- baking pan (about 9 x 13 x 2 inches deep)
- electric fan
- thermometer
- water at about room temperature
- table

Place the pan on the table and fill it about half full of water (Fig. 11-1). Measure the temperature of the water (Fig. 11-2). Now place the fan on the table so that it blows across the water. **Keep the fan itself away from the water. Electricity and water can be very dangerous. NEVER let electricity come into contact with water**. Turn on the fan (Fig. 11-3) and measure the temperature of the water again (Fig. 11-4). It should become cooler.

The molecules (tiny particles) that make up water are constantly moving. Some of them escape from the surface of the water into the air above. This happens during normal evaporation, but when the air above the water is moving, more molecules escape. The temperature of the water becomes cooler because the heat is absorbed from the water as it evaporates. The more rapid the evaporation, the greater the cooling.

Fig. 11-1. *Fill the pan about half full of water.*

Fig. 11-2. *Measure the temperature of the water.*

Fig. 11-3. *Blow a stream of air over the water.*

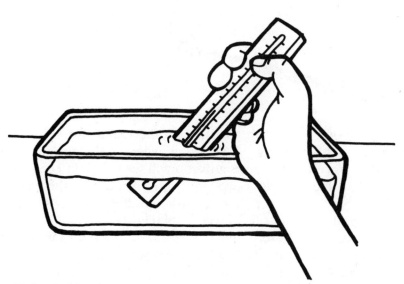

Fig. 11-4. *Air blowing over water lowers the temperature of the water.*

12

Comfort and Humidity

Materials

- Plastic bag or empty bread wrapper
- tape
- water at about room temperature

Place one hand in the plastic bag and seal it snugly around your arm with tape (Fig. 12-1). Try to make the bag airtight. Leave the bag in place a few minutes and you will see your hand begin to sweat and become wet. Now, wet your other hand with the warm water. Both hands are wet, but the one in the bag feels uncomfortable while the other hand feels cool (Fig. 12-2).

Humidity is a term that describes the amount of water vapor in the air. If the air contains a lot of moisture, the humidity is said to be high. When it contains only a little moisture, the humidity is low. When the air holds as much moisture as it can, and at a certain temperature and pressure, the air is saturated, or at the dew point.

The amount of moisture in the air compared to the amount required for saturation is called the relative humidity. That is, when the air contains only half of the moisture it can hold, the relative humidity is 50 percent.

Your hand in the bag feels sticky and uncomfortable because the humidity is too high. This keeps the perspiration from evaporating and cooling your skin like the moisture on your other hand.

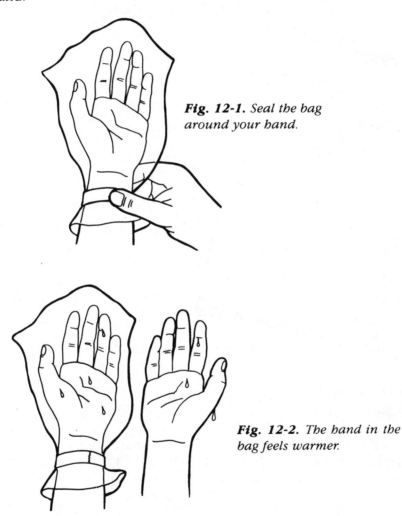

Fig. 12-1. Seal the bag around your hand.

Fig. 12-2. The hand in the bag feels warmer.

13

Why You See Your Breath on a Cold Day

Materials

• drinking glass
• ice cubes

Fill the glass about half full of ice cubes (Fig. 13-1) and gently blow over the rim of the glass (Fig. 13-2). You will see your breath coming up from inside the glass.

The air you breathe out from your lungs is warm and moist. The ice cubes cooled this air, much like a cold day. Cold air cannot hold as much moisture as warm air, so some of the moisture in your breath condensed into tiny droplets that you can see.

Fig. 13-1. Place a few ice cubes in a glass.

Fig. 13-2. Gently blow over the top of the glass.

14

Why Lakes Don't Freeze Solid

Materials

- clear glass bowl
- water
- refrigerator (freezing compartment)

Place a bowl about half full of water in the freezing compartment of the refrigerator (Fig. 14-1). Let it stand until ice forms on the surface. Remove the bowl and examine the ice (Fig. 14-2). You will see that the water expanded, or spread out, when it froze. The expanded ice on top of the water is less dense than the water below because it is spread out more. This makes the ice form on the surface.

Water is one of the few things that expands when it freezes. Most things contract, or get smaller, when their temperature is lowered and expand when they are heated. At temperatures above

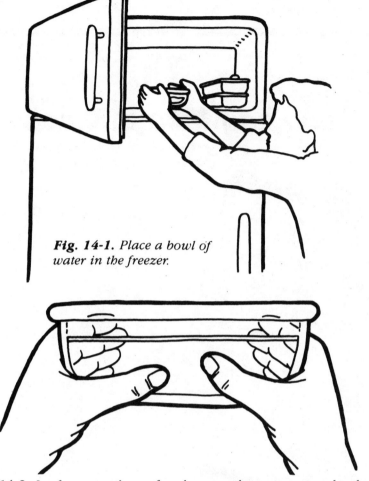

Fig. 14-1. *Place a bowl of water in the freezer.*

Fig. 14-2. *Ice forms on the surface because the water expands when it freezes.*

32 degrees, the molecules that make up water are always in motion. When the temperature drops, the molecules begin to slow down until the water reaches 32 degrees. At this point, the molecules almost stop moving and crystallize into ice.

The ice floats on the water and the surface of the water freezes. As the ice thickens, it insulates the water below it and keeps the water at a temperature above freezing. If it did not float, ice that formed in cold weather would sink and rivers, lakes, and even a large part of the ocean would freeze solid in winter. Fish could not live and there would be very little other water life.

15

How to Make a Rainbow

Materials

- garden hose with spray nozzle
- sunlight

Adjust the spray on the hose to a fine mist. Turn your back to the sun and spray the water up in the air in front of you. You should see an arch of brilliant colors (Fig. 15-1).

Rainbows are formed by the sun's rays when they are bent as they strike the drops of water. Rainbows give off seven colors: violet, indigo, blue, green, yellow, orange, and red. You can only see the colors that bend in your direction.

The height of a rainbow depends on how high the sun is. The higher the sun, the lower the rainbow. If the sun is higher than 40 degrees, you will be unable to see a rainbow.

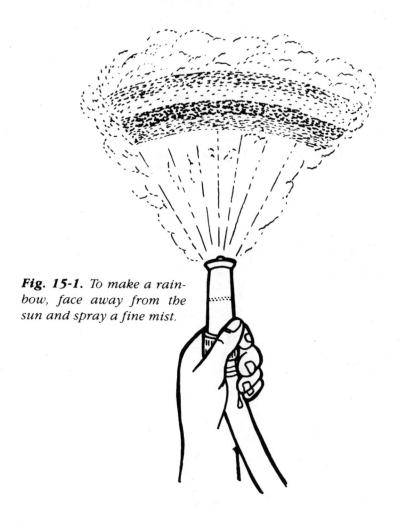

Fig. 15-1. To make a rainbow, face away from the sun and spray a fine mist.

16

Cloud Formations

Materials

- notebook
- pencil
- several cloudy days

Watch the clouds and see if you can break them down into these four groups:

1. Stratus clouds normally form only a few 100 feet above the ground. They are thin, billowy, foglike clouds that you sometimes see filling valleys. They are usually seen in early morning or late evening when the air is still (Fig. 16-1). The air often becomes calm at this time of day. The angle of the sun is low enough that the sun's energy is not heating the earth and creating winds.

STRATUS

Fig. 16-1. *Top view of stratus clouds.*

2. Cumulus clouds are fluffy white clouds that drift across the sky about a mile above the earth (Fig. 16-2). On a summer day, they make fast-moving shadows across the ground. They increase in numbers and become larger as the sun reaches its warmest in the afternoon. By evening, they usually thin and flatten into stratus clouds. A large number of heavy, cumulus clouds often means rain is in the forecast.

3. Nimbus clouds are dark gray clouds. They are the rain clouds. They tend to have shapeless formations and often blanket the sky. The bottom half of the cloud is filled with moisture that usually turns into raindrops (Fig. 16-3).

4. Cirrus clouds are feathery, white clouds that are made up of ice crystals (Fig. 16-4). They are the highest clouds in the sky, sometimes rising as high as 10 miles above the earth.

CUMULUS

Fig. 16-2. *Cumulus clouds become larger in the afternoon.*

NIMBUS

Fig. 16-3. *Nimbus clouds often mean rain is coming.*

CIRRUS

Fig. 16-4. *Cirrus clouds are high, feathery clouds.*

Clouds are often classified into four groups according to the heights at which they form.

1. Stratocumulus. Stratocumulus are rain clouds that range from near the ground to about 6,500 feet (Fig. 16-5).

2. Altostratus. Altostratus is a thick, blue-gray cloud blanket that is found from 6,500 feet to 20,000 feet (Fig. 16-6).

3. Altocumulus. Altocumulus clouds are made up of small, white or gray cumulus clouds (Fig. 16-7). These small cumulus clouds are packed close together and form a gray mass that can be found at heights of 8,000 to 20,000 feet.

4. Cumulonimbus. Cumulonimbus clouds are often called thunderheads. They are giant, cauliflower-shaped clouds that can reach heights of up to 11 miles (Fig. 16-8). These towering clouds usually bring thunderstorms with rain, snow, or hail.

STRATOCUMULUS

Fig. 16-5. *Stratocumulus clouds are water-droplet clouds.*

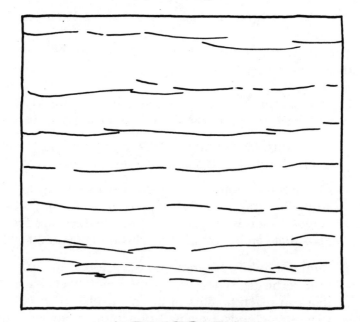

ALTOSTRATUS

Fig. 16-6. *Altostratus clouds form thick, blue-gray blankets.*

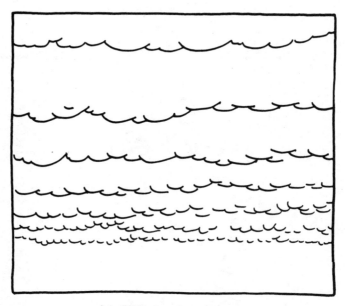

ALTOCUMULUS

Fig. 16-7. *Altocumulus clouds are round, white, or grayish masses of small cumulus clouds.*

CUMULONIMBUS

Fig. 16-8. *Cumulonimbus clouds can be found at all cloud levels.*

17
Dew Point

Materials

- tin can or metal cup
- thermometer
- tablespoon
- ice cubes
- paper towel
- bowl
- cool water
- salt

The ice cubes should be broken into smaller pieces. Lay the paper towel across one hand and place an ice cube on the towel. Hit the ice cube sharply with the back side of the spoon (Fig. 17-1). The ice cube will shatter into smaller pieces. Place these pieces into the bowl. Continue breaking the ice until you have about half a bowl full of crushed ice.

Make sure that the outside of the can is dry and then fill it about one-fourth full of cool water (Fig. 17-2). Place the thermometer in the can. Add a tablespoon of crushed ice (Fig. 17-3) and stir. Continue to slowly add ice and stir until a thin layer of moisture, or

Fig. 17-1. *Strike the ice cube with the spoon.*

Fig. 17-2. *Add a little cool water to the can.*

dew, forms on the outside of the can. Read the temperature at the instant the dew forms (Fig. 17-4). This is the dew point. Add salt to the ice and continue stirring (Fig. 17-5). The moisture will turn into frost because the salt lowered the temperature of the dew to freezing.

Meteorologists find the dew point of air by cooling the air until its water vapor begins to condense. The dew point temperature is not a fixed temperature but changes from day to day. It depends on the amount of moisture in the air.

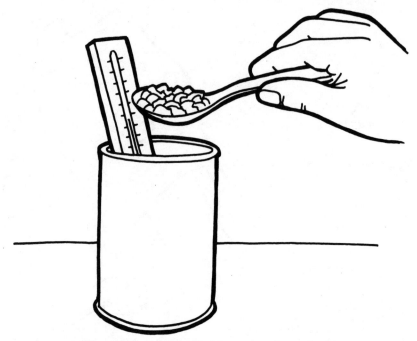

Fig. 17-3. *Add one tablespoon of crushed ice.*

Fig. 17-4. *The dew point is the temperature reading the instant moisture forms.*

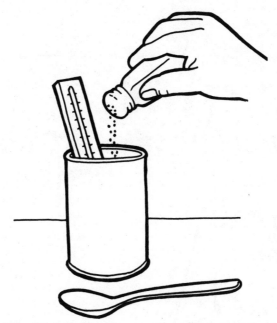

Fig. 17-5. *Salt will cause the moisture to freeze.*

18

How to Make a Cloud

Materials

- glass jug with a small mouth
- match or candle

Turn the jug upside down and carefully hold the opening over the flame of a match or candle (Fig. 18-1). Warm the air inside the jug a few seconds then quickly place your mouth inside the opening to make a seal, then blow hard into the jug (Fig. 18-2). Compress the air inside the jug as much as possible, but be careful not to breathe in. Now, quickly remove your mouth and release the pressure. A cloud will form inside the jug (Fig. 18-3).

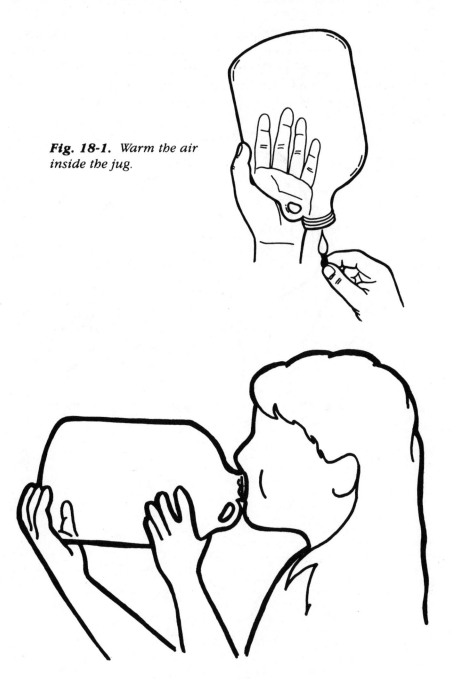

Fig. 18-1. *Warm the air inside the jug.*

Fig. 18-2. *Compress the air inside the jug.*

When you compressed the air in the jug, you also added moisture from your breath. When you suddenly released the pressure, the air in the jug expanded and cooled. The air couldn't hold as much moisture as the warmer air and some of the moisture condensed into tiny droplets and formed a cloud.

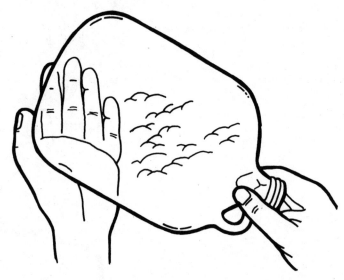

Fig. 18-3. *The air expands and cools, forming a cloud.*

19

How to Make Fog

Materials
- clear glass jar
- tea strainer
- ice cubes
- hot water

Fill the jar about half full of hot water (Fig. 19-1). Place the tea strainer over the opening so that the opening is filled (Fig. 19-2). Fill the tea strainer with ice cubes (Fig. 19-3), and fog will form inside the jar (Fig. 19-4).

The warm air from the water was cooled by the air from the ice. The warm air was saturated with moisture and was cooled below its dew point. Water vapor then condensed into tiny drops of water that were suspended in the air and a fog formed. Fog is just a cloud close to the ground.

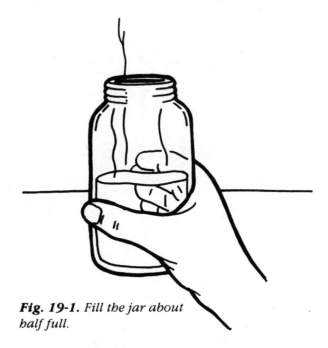

Fig. 19-1. Fill the jar about half full.

Fig. 19-2. Put the tea strainer on top.

Fig. 19-3. *Add a few ice cubes.*

Fig. 19-4. *Fog will form in the jar.*

20

How Water Gets into the Air

Materials

- 2 jars the same size (one with a lid)
- marking pencil
- water

Fill both jars about half full of water (Fig. 20-1). Mark the water level on each jar (Fig. 20-2). Put the lid on one of the jars and leave the other jar open (Fig. 20-3). Let the jars stand side by side for several days. Check the water levels each day and mark any changes in the level. The water level in the open jar will keep falling (Fig. 20-4). Which jar has the air that contains the most water vapor? Is this air saturated?

Water does not evaporate at the same rate every day. It depends on the temperature of the air. The air in the sealed jar became saturated, and when the air is saturated, no more water can evaporate in that air. The warmer the air, the more moisture it can hold. For example, a cubic foot of saturated air at 90 degrees contains five times as much moisture as saturated air at 40 degrees.

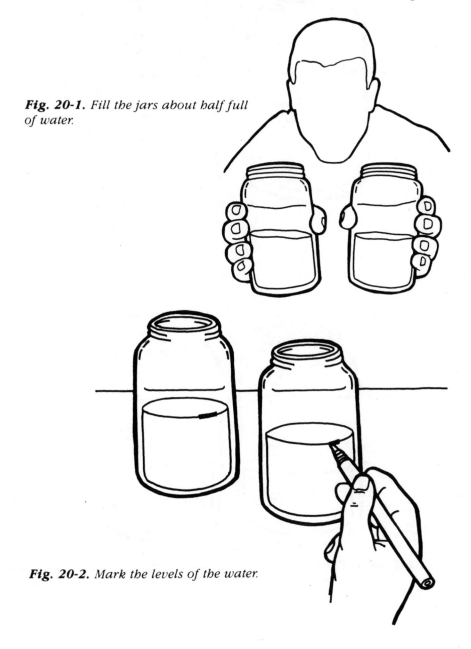

Fig. 20-1. *Fill the jars about half full of water.*

Fig. 20-2. *Mark the levels of the water.*

Fig. 20-3. *Put the lid on one of the jars.*

Fig. 20-4. *Water does not evaporate when the air becomes saturated.*

PART IV

GEOLOGY

1
Soil Erosion

Materials

- a small area of bare soil
- an equal area of soil with grass
- water hose with adjustable nozzle

Adjust the nozzle of the water hose to a spray similar to rainfall, and spray the bare soil a few minutes. Soon gullies will form, and the soil will begin to wash away. Now spray the grassy area for about the same period of time. You will see a little of the soil washing away. The blades of grass soften the fall of water, and the roots help hold the soil together. You also can make furrows along the contours of the bare ground to prevent the soil from washing away and to conserve water for plants.

Erosion is the wearing away of the earth. It is mostly caused by wind and water. Large, deep-rooted trees have been slowly buried and killed by wind-blown sand, and farms have been abandoned after the fertile soil was washed away by wind or rain.

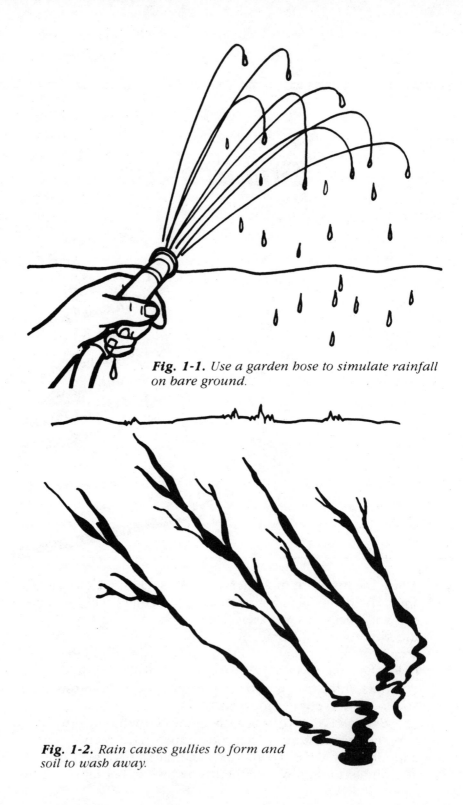

Fig. 1-1. Use a garden hose to simulate rainfall on bare ground.

Fig. 1-2. Rain causes gullies to form and soil to wash away.

Fig. 1-3. *Grass softens the force of rain and helps hold the soil together.*

2

How Rocks Can Be Squeezed and Folded

Materials

- modeling clay (3 different colors)
- tablespoon

Roll each color clay into strips and build up layers of different colors. Push the layers from the ends until they start to fold. The shallow, up and down folds are called *upright anticlines* and *synclines*. Continue pushing from the ends until a fold begins to roll over. This fold is called an *overfold*. If you keep pushing and the layers begin to tear, it will become a faulted fold or a thrust-faulted fold. Now use the spoon to carve formations in the clay such as mountains and valleys. You will see how the different layers of rock make the various patterns often seen where highways are cut through mountains.

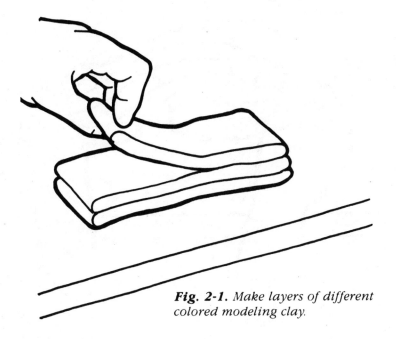

Fig. 2-1. *Make layers of different colored modeling clay.*

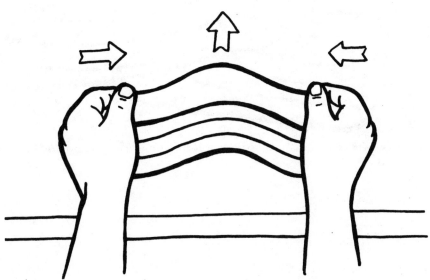

Fig. 2-2. *Push the layers together from the ends to make the folds called anticlines and synclines.*

Fig. 2-3. *Continued pressure from the ends will cause an overfold.*

Fig. 2-4. *If pressure continues until the fold tears, it is called a faulted fold.*

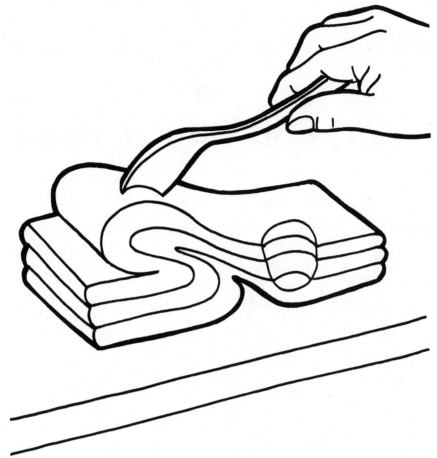

Fig. 2-5. *Sections cut from the clay will show patterns similar to those found in layers of rock.*

3
Why Rocks Break Apart

Materials

- Small glass bottle with screw-on lid
- Paper towels
- refrigerator
- water

Fill the bottle completely full of water and screw the lid on tightly. Wrap a couple of paper towels around the bottle and place the bottle in the freezing compartment of a refrigerator over night. Now carefully unfold the paper towels and examine the bottle. It will be broken in several pieces. When the water froze, it expanded and broke the bottle. After you have finished, throw the towels and broken glass in the trash.

Water often seeps into the cracks in a rock. If the water freezes, it will expand with a tremendous force and cause the cracks to grow bigger and longer. This expansion force can break rocks into smaller pieces.

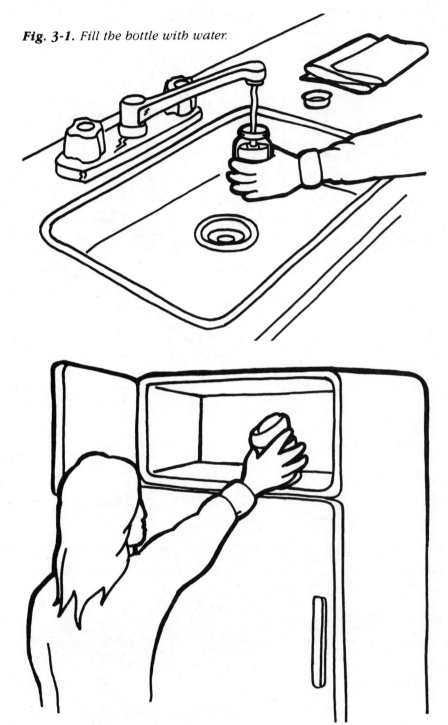

Fig. 3-1. Fill the bottle with water.

Fig. 3-2. Wrap paper towels around the bottle and place it in the freezer.

Fig. 3-3. *When the water froze it expanded.*

Fig. 3-4. *Cracks in rocks often contain moisture. If it freezes, it can split the rocks.*

Sun shining on a rock will cause the surface of the rock to get hotter than the inner part of the rock. This heat makes the outer part of the rock expand more than the inside part. This expansion can cause the rock to crack. At night, the outer part of the rock cools faster than the inner part. This cooling causes the outer part to contract more than the inside, and more cracks can form. You might have seen places where large sheets of rock have split away and tumbled down the side of a hill.

4

Materials in Soil

Spread a little soil on the paper and examine it with the magnifying glass. Look for small pieces of sand, humus, and clay. The sand will be in the form of tiny grains of glasslike particles that can have sharp or rounded corners. *Humus* is a brown or black substance that forms from the partial decay of plant or animal matter. It is the organic part of the soil. Clay is usually lighter than the color of humus. It might be too fine for you to see with a magnifying glass.

Soil is made up of sand or clay, or both, mixed with humus. Often the top layer of soil, called the *topsoil*, contains a lot of humus. The layer of soil just below the topsoil is called the *subsoil*. It usually contains little or no humus.

Fig. 4-1. *Spread a little soil on a white paper.*

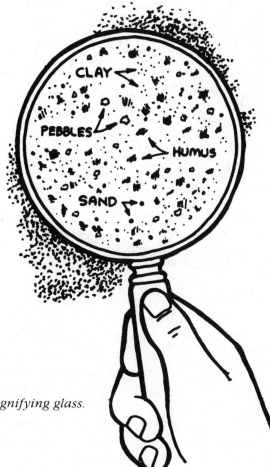

Fig. 4-2. *Examine the soil with a magnifying glass.*

5
How Plants Break Up Rocks

Materials

- cardboard box
  (lid from shoe box)
- plaster of paris
- paper towels
- lima bean seeds
- water

Mix the plaster of paris with water until you have a creamy mixture. Pour this mixture into the box. Now lay a few lima bean seeds on top of the wet plaster. Spread them around so that they're not too close. Next, cover the seeds with layers of wet paper towels. Wet the towels occasionally to keep them moist for about a week.

After a week, check the growth of the beans and the condition of the plaster. Remove a couple of the seeds and notice what happened to the plaster. Wait a couple of more days and examine the seeds and plaster again. Continue to watch the growth of the seeds, and you will see the roots of the sprouts dig into the plaster to get minerals. The plaster is a form of rock. The roots, searching for food, help break up rocks.

Fig. 5-1. *Pour plaster of paris into the box.*

Fig. 5-2. *Place lima beans on top of the wet plaster.*

Fig. 5-3. *Cover the beans with wet paper towels.*

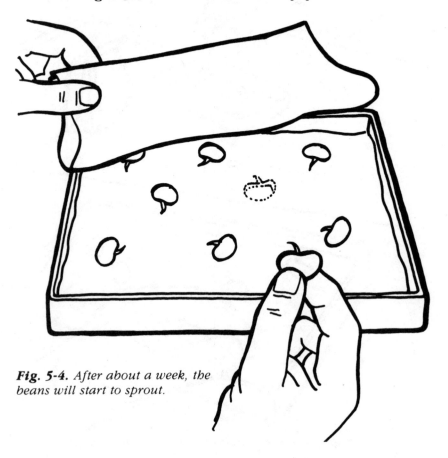

Fig. 5-4. *After about a week, the beans will start to sprout.*

Fig. 5-5. *The roots grow into the plaster and are strong enough to break it.*

6

How Water Separates Materials

Materials

- soil
- clear, glass jar
- water
- spoon

Fill the jar about one-third full of soil. Fill the jar the rest of the way up with water. Stir the water vigorously and let it stand a few days.

After the water has settled completely, and if the soil is rich, you will find the soil has been separated into layers. The top of the soil might have a thin layer of black carbon from the humus. The next layer down will contain fine mud, followed by grit and then small gravel at the bottom. Similar layers often can be found in sandstone.

Fig. 6-1. Fill the jar part way with soil.

Fig. 6-2. Fill the rest of the jar with water and stir vigorously.

Fig. 6-3. When settling, the water separates the soil into layers.

WATER

CARBON
FINE MUD

SILT

GRIT

SMALL
GRAVEL

7

Geology in Your Neighborhood

Look for older public buildings in your neighborhood: schools, libraries, banks, or churches. Some might be made from local stone, but often polished, imported granite is used in banks and office buildings. Parks sometimes have statues made from fine marble. You also might find other decorative stones such as granite and limestone. Make a list of the different types of stone you find and try to learn where they came from. You might also want to note if any weathering has affected the stone and what caused the wear.

Fig. 7-1. *Statues and old buildings often are made from rocks such as marble and granite.*

Fig. 7-2. *Use a magnifying glass to examine the stones.*

Fig. 7-3. *A list will help you keep track of the different types of stones you find.*

8

Testing Water for Minerals

Materials
- tap water
- rainwater or distilled water
- 2 saucers
- 2 jars with lids
- magnifying glass
- medicine dropper

Fill one jar with tap water and the other jar with rainwater. Now place several drops of tap water on one saucer and about the same amount of rainwater in the other saucer. Set both saucers aside until the water evaporates. Now use the magnifying glass to examine the rings left by the water. You will see that the tap water contained more minerals than the rainwater.

When water falls as rain, it contains no dissolved solid matter. Some of it runs off and finds its way into streams and rivers and eventually makes its way into lakes and oceans. The ground soaks up some of the water. Layers of clay or sand and the cracks in rocks store large amounts of water. Some of this water might have been locked under the ground for thousands of years. It could have

Fig. 8-1. *Place drops of different types of water on saucers.*

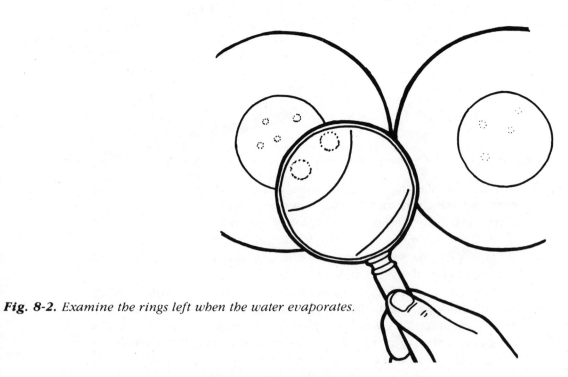

Fig. 8-2. *Examine the rings left when the water evaporates.*

Fig. 8-3. *Water makes a cycle between the oceans, clouds, rain, and then back to the oceans again.*

fallen as rain before the time of humans. Our water is continually making a cycle between the oceans, clouds, rain, streams, rivers, and lakes then back to the oceans again. It only changes its form and moves from place to place.

Because water dissolves many substances, a large number of these substances usually are present in natural water. The most common impurities are compounds of the chemicals: sodium, calcium, magnesium, and iron. Fortunately, these chemicals are not harmful to humans in small quantities.

9

Testing Water for Hardness

Materials

- tap water
- rainwater or distilled water
- 2 jars with lids
- medicine dropper
- liquid detergent
- pencil and paper
- spoon
- washing soda

Fill one jar about two-thirds full of tap water and pour an equal amount of rainwater into the other jar. Use the medicine dropper and add 2 drops of detergent to the tap water. Screw the lid on tight and shake the jar. If the detergent doesn't lather, add 2 more drops of detergent and shake the jar again. Continue to add detergent until it lathers. Now count the number of drops the water needed to produce a lather.

Repeat the same test with the rainwater and compare the number of drops of detergent used in each jar.

The water that required the most detergent is called *hard water*. This water should have been the tap water. Water that requires little soap to lather is called *soft water*.

Fig. 9-1. *Fill jars with equal amounts of tap water and rainwater.*

Fig. 9-2. *Add two drops of detergent to the tap water.*

Fig. 9-3. *Shake the jar to make a lather.*

Fig. 9-4. *Compare the number of drops of detergent required to make both types of water lather.*

Fig. 9-5. *Washing soda helps hard water produce a lather.*

Calcium salts in the tap water keep the soap from lathering. If you add washing soda (sodium carbonate) to the tap water, the carbonate part of the soda mixes with the calcium in the water, making calcium carbonate. Now the calcium cannot react with the soap, and the soap can lather.

10
The Salty Ocean

Materials

- cup
- glass
- teaspoon
- tablespoon
- 1 teaspoon of table salt
- 10 tablespoons of water

Pour 1 teaspoon of salt into the cup and add 10 tablespoons of water. Stir the mixture thoroughly. Wet your finger in the water and taste the solution. This solution is about the same mixture as sea water. Ocean water contains about 3.5 percent salts; mostly, sodium chloride (table salt), potassium, and calcium salts along with magnesium salts. Every stream and river that flows into the ocean carries some amount of salt dissolved in it. It has been estimated that one-fourth of the material that the Mississippi River alone deposits in the sea is dissolved minerals. Small plants and animals, called *plankton*, use some of the salts. Chemical action of the sea water and sediment on the ocean floor also removes some of the salt, but very little of the sodium chloride is taken from the water.

Fig. 10-1. *Pour a teaspoon of salt into the cup.*

Fig. 10-2. *Add ten tablespoons of water.*

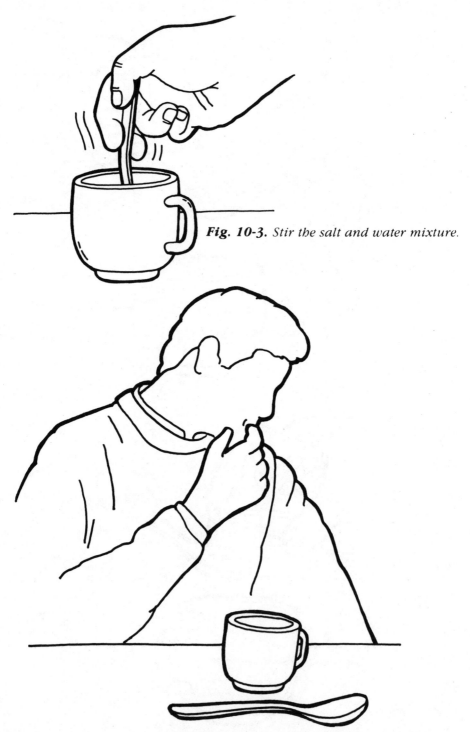

Fig. 10-3. *Stir the salt and water mixture.*

Fig. 10-4. *Taste the solution. It is about the same mixture as sea water.*

11
Looking at Salt

Materials
- table salt
- magnifying glass
- piece of paper

Sprinkle a few grains of salt on the paper and examine them with the magnifying glass. You will see tiny cubelike crystals. The crystals are not transparent because of impurities. These crystals will not absorb water easily. Sometimes, however, tiny amounts of other minerals become mixed with the salt and they absorb moisture from the air. For this reason, on humid days, salt in a salt shaker becomes moist and lumpy.

Fig. 11-1. Sprinkle a few grains of salt on a paper.

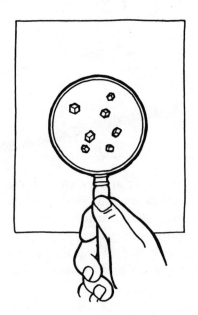

Fig. 11-2. Examine the crystals with a magnifying glass.

12
How Salt Crystals Form

Materials
- 3 tablespoons of soil
- 2 tablespoons of table salt
- ½ cup of water
- saucer
- glass
- tablespoon
- magnifying glass

Spread about 3 tablespoons of soil out in the saucer. Fill the glass about half full of water and add 2 tablespoons of salt. Stir the water several minutes to dissolve most of the salt. Let the water settle and then pour some of the clear salt water over the soil. Set the saucer in a warm place until the water evaporates and the mud is dry. Now examine the soil. At first, it might look like the tops of the small rocks were dusted with frost, but under the magnifying glass, you will see that they are topped by large crystals of salt called *rock salt*. More crystals will cover the rest of the soil. Rock salt is formed when minerals are dissolved in water. The salt water is drawn up through small openings in the soil and rocks by capillary action.

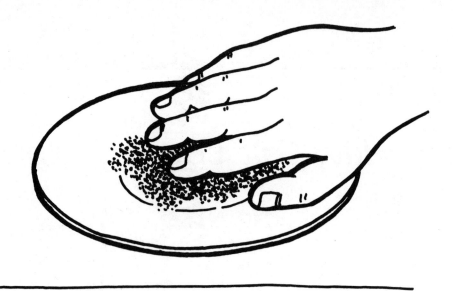

Fig. 12-1. *Place a little soil in a saucer and spread it out.*

Fig. 12-2. *Add two tablespoons of salt to a half glass of water.*

The water then evaporates into the air leaving the salt behind. As the water evaporates, the molecules in the salt start to cling together and grow into larger crystals. The slower the evaporation, the larger the crystals.

Rock salt is made up of the mineral halite. It forms after long periods of evaporation of sea and lake water in an arid climate. Salt beds in such humid areas as New York, Ohio, and Michigan mean that the climate of those areas has changed since the beds were deposited.

Fig. 12-3. *Stir the water until most of the salt dissolves.*

Fig. 12-4. *Wet the soil with the salt water.*

Fig. 12-5. Allow the mud to dry.

Fig. 12-6. Examine the soil for salt crystals.

13
The Differences Between Rocks and Minerals

Materials
- Salt crystal
- quartz crystal
- piece of granite
- magnifying glass

Examine the salt crystal under the magnifying glass, and then examine the quartz crystal. Now look at the piece of granite. Compare the differences you see. The salt and quartz are minerals. The piece of granite is a rock. Minerals are the building blocks that make up rock. Some minerals are made from only one element, while others might consist of a complicated mixture of elements. Their individual make-up, however, is always the same. Table salt always has one atom of sodium for each atom of chlorine. Quartz is always made up of two-thirds oxygen and one-third silicon. Rocks, however, are almost always made up of a mixture of minerals.

Because rocks are formed in different ways than minerals, their mixtures can vary. The piece of granite probably consists of about 75 percent feldspar, about 20 percent quartz, and about 5 percent mica. Unlike minerals, the proportions do vary, and rocks can consist also of small amounts of other minerals.

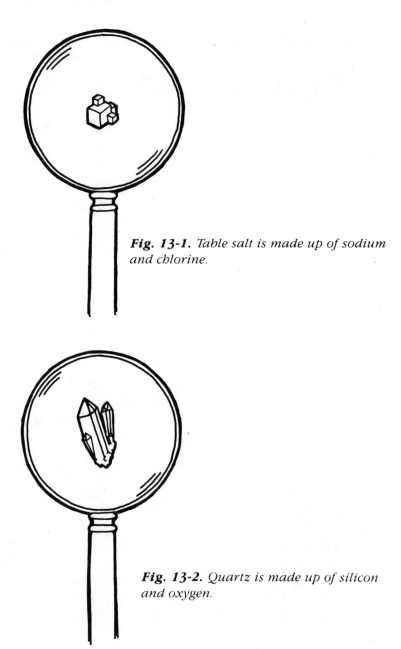

Fig. 13-1. Table salt is made up of sodium and chlorine.

Fig. 13-2. Quartz is made up of silicon and oxygen.

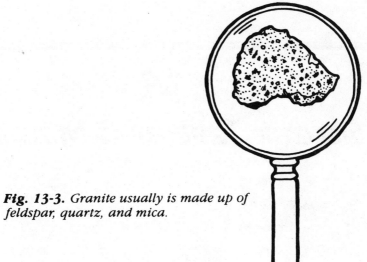

Fig. 13-3. Granite usually is made up of feldspar, quartz, and mica.

14
Streak Test of a Mineral

Materials

- piece of quartz
- piece of ceramic tile

To test the streak of the quartz, carefully scratch a mark across the back, (the dull, unglazed side), of the ceramic tile with the quartz. The streak will be white. The streak of a mineral is the color of its fine powder. It often is obtained by pulverizing the mineral on a piece of unglazed porcelain or by scratching the mineral with a knife or file. The streak of the quartz was white, but often the color of the streak will be very different from the color of the un-powdered mineral.

For example, the mineral hematite is black but has a red streak. The streak of a particular mineral is almost always the same color even though the body color of the mineral varies. For example, the transparent, crystalline mineral fluorite is found in many colors; yellow, green, violet, blue, brown, black, and colorless, but all will have a white streak.

Fig. 14-1. *To streak test, scratch a mark across the back of a piece of ceramic tile.*

15
How to Grow Crystals

Materials

- 10-12 ounces of white alum (from grocery store)
- 1 pint of water
- stove
- pot
- bowl
- spoon
- cup
- tissue paper

Pour the pint of water into the pot and then add about 5 ounces of alum. Have an adult help you heat the water on the stove but don't allow it to boil. Stir the water until the alum dissolves. Continue to add more alum, a little at a time, and stir until no more alum will dissolve. You then will have what is called a saturated solution. Carefully remove the pot from the stove and pour half of the solution into the bowl. Use pot holders or protective gloves. Hot solution can burn!

Set the bowl aside for a few days. Pour the rest of the solution into the jar, leaving any settled material in the pot. Cover the jar with the card to keep out dust particles. After a few days, small crystals will appear in the bowl. Leave them until they are about

Fig. 15-1. *Pour about a pint of water into a pot.*

Fig. 15-2. *Add about five ounces of alum.*

Fig. 15-3. *Heat the water but don't let it boil. Add more alum.*

Fig. 15-4. *Pour some of the solution into a bowl and set it aside.*

Fig. 15-5. *Pour the rest of the solution into a jar, leaving settled material in the pot.*

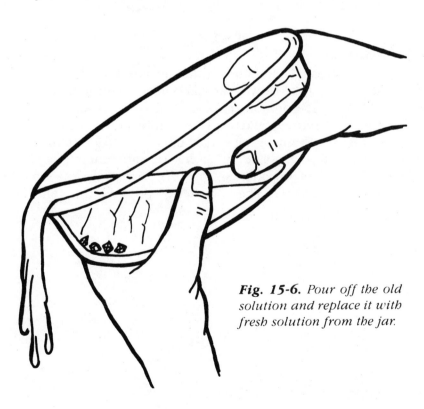

Fig. 15-6. *Pour off the old solution and replace it with fresh solution from the jar.*

Fig. 15-7. *Examine the crystals with a magnifying glass.*

$1/8$ inch across. Then pour off the old solution and dry the crystals with tissue paper. Now pour some fresh solution from the jar into the bowl. Place one of the best crystals in the solution and allow the bowl to set several days. Then remove the crystal and dry it on tissue paper. Examine the crystal under the magnifying glass.

Minerals are made of atoms of different elements packed together in certain patterns. This pattern is always the same for that particular mineral. These patterns provide different types of crystals with their distinctive shape.

16
Testing Chalk with an Acid

Materials

- piece of school chalk
- medicine dropper
- vinegar
- knife or single-edged safety razor blade
- plate

Have an adult help you scrape some chalk powder into a small mound and drop a few drops of vinegar on it. Always be very careful with sharp objects!

You will notice that the chalk powder does not bubble. School chalk is made mostly of gypsum. Strong acids will react with gypsum, but weak acids, like vinegar, cause little or no reaction.

Fig. 16-1. Scrape some chalk powder into a mound.

Fig. 16-2. Add a few drops of vinegar.

17

Hardness Test for Chalk

Materials

- piece of school chalk
- your fingernail

Try to make a scratch or groove in the chalk with your fingernail. You should be able to do this easily.

Minerals often are classified by their hardness in numbers from 1 to 10, with 10 being the hardest. A diamond is the hardest mineral, classified with a number 10. Your fingernail has a hardness of about 2.5; it should be harder than the chalk, which has a hardness of 2. A mineral will make a scratch or mark on anything that is of the same hardness, or less hardness, than itself.

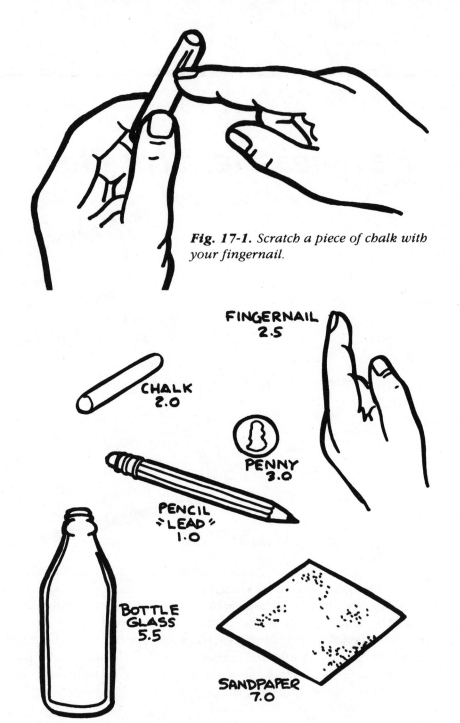

Fig. 17-1. Scratch a piece of chalk with your fingernail.

FINGERNAIL
2.5

CHALK
2.0

PENNY
3.0

PENCIL
"LEAD"
1.0

BOTTLE
GLASS
5.5

SANDPAPER
7.0

Fig. 17-2. Minerals are classified by their hardness in numbers from one to ten.

18
How to Make Gypsum

Materials

- 1 cup of plaster of paris
- ½ cup of water
- spoon
- bowl for mixing
- small bowl
- 2 tablespoons of cooking oil or grease

Pour 1 cup of plaster of paris into the mixing bowl and add ½ cup of water. Stir the mixture until it becomes a smooth, thick paste. Wipe the inside of the small bowl with a thin film of oil to keep the plaster from sticking. Now pour the mixture into the bowl and wait until it hardens. This procedure might take about 30 minutes.

When you heat gypsum, it loses three-fourths of its water. This process is called *calcination*. It changes the gypsum into the fine, white powder called plaster of paris. When you add water to the powder, it turns back into gypsum.

Fig. 18-1. *Pour plaster of paris into a mixing bowl.*

Fig. 18-2. *Add about half as much water.*

Fig. 18-3. *Stir the mixture until it becomes smooth.*

OIL

Fig. 18-4. *Apply a thin film of oil to the other bowl to prevent sticking.*

Fig. 18-5. *Pour the mixture into the oiled bowl.*

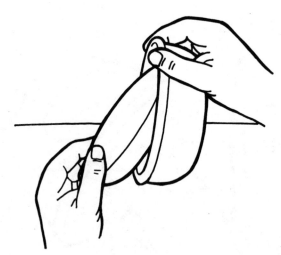

Fig. 18-6. *The mixture will harden and turn into gypsum.*

Gypsum is a white or yellowish-white mineral used to make plaster of paris. When water evaporates from solutions of the mineral, large deposits of gypsum are formed. It is mined to make various products including plaster, cement, and paints.

19

Hardness Test for Gypsum

Materials
- piece of gypsum
- your fingernail

Try to make a scratch in the gypsum with your fingernail. You should be able to do this, because gypsum has a hardness of 2.

Gypsum might form transparent, colorless crystals called *selenite*, or it might be in a fine, white fibrous mass with a satiny luster called *satin spar*. Alabaster is another variety of gypsum that often is used for statuary and other carvings. Another form of gypsum is called rock gypsum. It is similar to alabaster except that it has a dull luster and usually contains noticeable impurities. It is used in the production of plaster of paris. School chalk is made up of mostly gypsum.

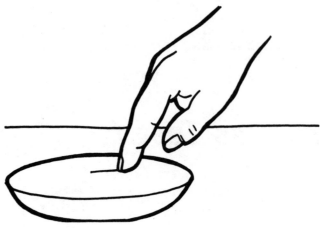

Fig. 19-1. *You should be able to scratch gypsum with your fingernail.*

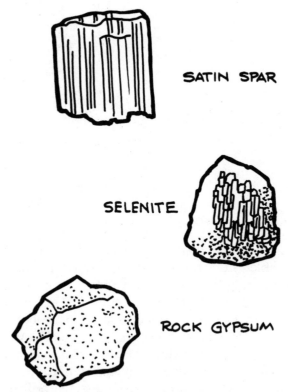

SATIN SPAR

SELENITE

ROCK GYPSUM

Fig. 19-2. *Gypsum can be found in different forms.*

PART V

ANIMAL BIOLOGY

1

Parts of an Insect

Examine the ant under the magnifying glass and notice it has six legs (Fig. 1-1). Look closely at the three parts of the jointed body. All mature insects have six legs and a jointed body. Creatures such as spiders, mites, ticks, and centipedes are not true insects.

The body is divided into three parts: the head, the middle body or *thorax*, and the abdomen (Fig. 1-2). The head contains its brain, its feelers or antennae, its eyes, and its mouth. The middle body contains the motor parts. It holds the main muscles that are used for walking, swimming, or flying. The legs, and any wings, are always connected to the middle body. The abdomen, at the rear of the insect, holds the digestive, reproductive, and other organs.

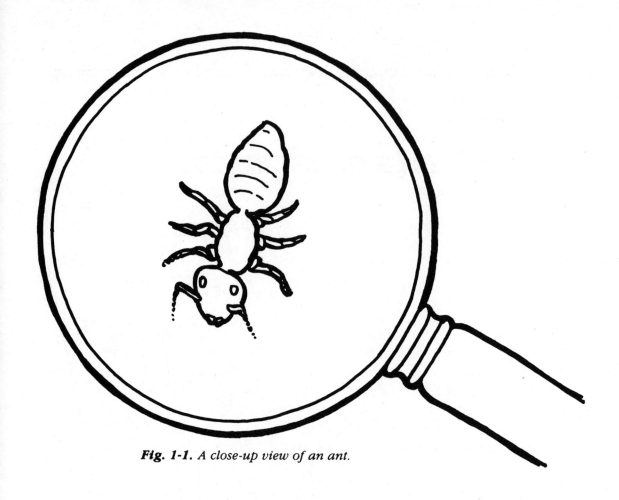

Fig. 1-1. *A close-up view of an ant.*

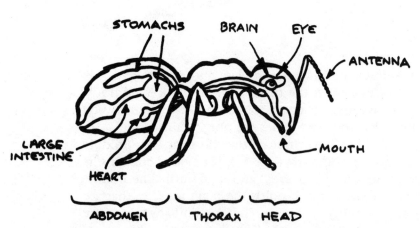

STOMACHS BRAIN EYE

ANTENNA

LARGE
INTESTINE

MOUTH

HEART

ABDOMEN THORAX HEAD

Fig. 1-2. *The body is made up of three parts.*

The outer body of an insect is made of a tough or horny material. This acts like a suit of armor and forms an outside skeleton. Insects have no internal framework of bones like we have. For an insect to grow, it must shed its outer skeleton and get a new and larger one.

The blood of an insect is normally yellowish, greenish, or colorless. It is pumped by the pulsating part of a tube-shaped blood vessel that extends the length of the body. This pumping part, called the *heart*, is located in the abdomen.

Insects have no lungs. They take in oxygen through small openings along the side of the body. All insects are coldblooded. This means that their body temperatures are about the same as their surroundings. Because of this, their activity depends a great deal on the temperature. Insects are more active on warm days.

2

Collecting Insects

Materials

- NETTING MATERIAL (CHEESE CLOTH)
- WIRE (FROM CLOTHES HANGER)
- OLD BROOM HANDLE
- TAPE (FRICTION OR DUCT)

You can purchase a collecting net at some hobby stores (about $6.00 or $7.00), or you can make your own out of netting material. Bend the wire into a loop about 12 or 14 inches in diameter. Form the loop in the middle of the wire. Leave the ends of the wire bent down to fasten to the broom handle (Fig. 2-1). Tape the wire ends securely to the end of the broom handle (Fig. 2-2). You may need adult help to form a sock about 2 feet long from the netting material and use tape to fasten it to the wire loop (Fig. 2-3).

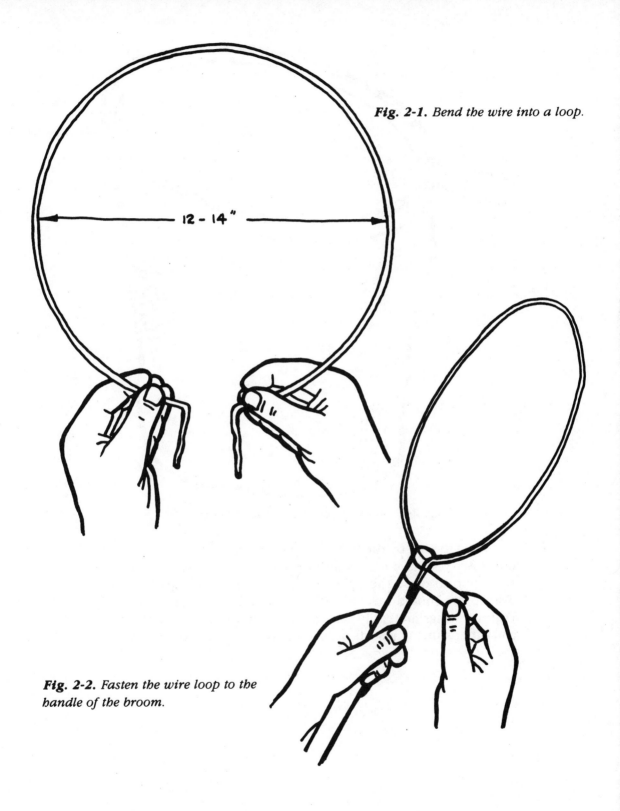

Fig. 2-1. *Bend the wire into a loop.*

12 – 14"

Fig. 2-2. *Fasten the wire loop to the handle of the broom.*

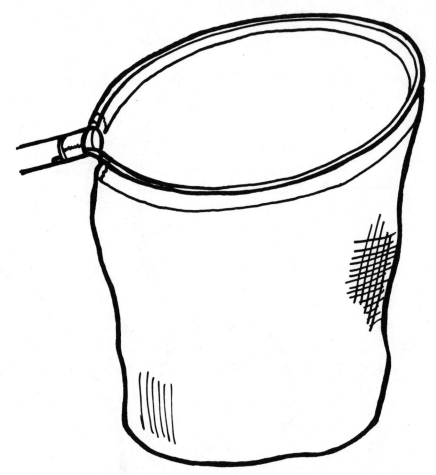

Fig. 2-3. *Attach the cheesecloth to the wire loop.*

Hold the net by the handle and swing it so that the net billows out. After you have caught an insect in the net, quickly rotate the wire loop to close the open end (Fig. 2-4). This traps the insect inside. You should now be able to transfer it to a jar. Be careful. Delicate wings are easily damaged. Be sure to avoid bees, wasps, and other stinging insects until you have a lot of experience.

Fig. 2-4. *Twist the handle to close off the net.*

3
A Jar For Killing Insects

Materials

- WIDE-MOUTH GLASS JAR WITH LID
- COTTON
- FINGERNAIL POLISH REMOVER OR COMMERCIAL INSECTICIDE
- SMALL PIECE OF SCREEN WIRE

Place a layer of cotton in the bottom of the jar. Cut the screen wire that is cut to fit the inside of the jar and lay it on top of the cotton (Fig. 3-1). Pour some nail polish remover over the cotton until the cotton is saturated (Fig. 3-2). Drop the insect in the jar and quickly screw the lid in place (Fig. 3-3). The fumes from the nail polish remover should kill the insect within a few minutes.

This experiment should be done to study the insects. The killing of any living organism should be done with much consideration.

Fig. 3-1. *Place the wire screen on top of the cotton.*

Fig. 3-2. *Saturate the cotton with nail polish remover.*

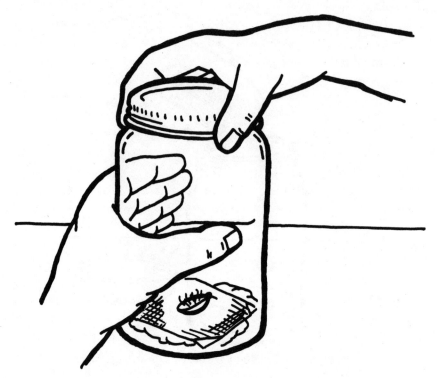

Fig. 3-3. *The lid will keep the fumes inside the jar.*

4

Collecting Crawling Insects

Materials

- WIDE-MOUTH GLASS JAR
- BOARD OR ROCK
- SHOVEL

Dig a small hole in the ground the size of the jar. Set the jar in the ground so that the rim is just below ground level. Fill in the area around the jar with dirt (Fig. 4-1). Place the board over the hole so that the board rests on the ground and not on the rim of the jar (Fig. 4-2). Insects like to hide under boards and rocks. When they fall into the jar, the slick sides prevent them from crawling back out. Check your trap every day and remove it when you are through collecting so no insects will die needlessly.

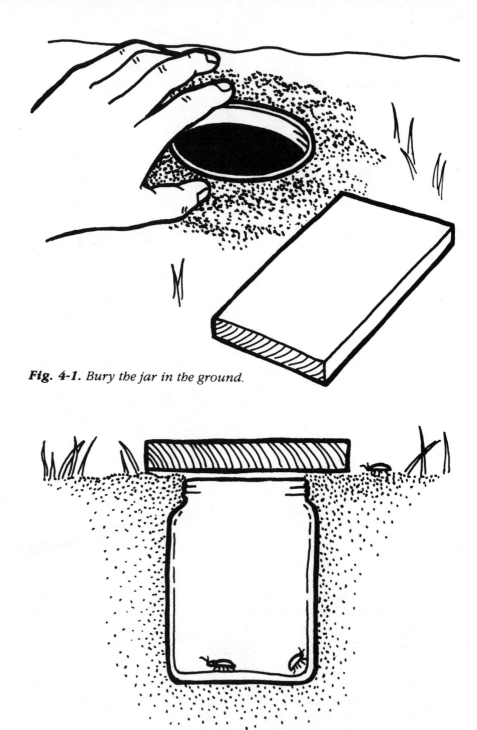

Fig. 4-1. *Bury the jar in the ground.*

Fig. 4-2. *Place the board over the jar.*

Be very careful. Use long tweezers or forceps when picking up insects (Fig. 4-3). Many insects can bite or sting. Some insects, like scorpions, should be avoided altogether or killed while they are still in the trap.

Fig. 4-3. *Use tweezers to pick up the insects.*

5

A Jar for Relaxing Insects

Materials

- WIDE-MOUTH GLASS JAR WITH LID
- COTTON
- WIRE SCREEN
- WATER

Place a layer of cotton in the bottom of the jar (Fig. 5-1) and put the wire screen on top, the same as the jar for studying dead insects. Only this time, soak the cotton with water (Fig. 5-2). When you find an insect that is already dead, place it in the jar (Fig. 5-3), replace the lid and let it set overnight (Fig. 5-4). The high humidity in the jar will relax the wings of butterflies, dragonflies, and other insects with large delicate wings.

Fig. 5-1. *Place cotton in the bottom of the jar.*

Fig. 5-2. *Saturate the cotton with water.*

Fig. 5-3. *Place the dead insect in the jar.*

RELAXING JAR

Fig. 5-4. *Let the jar set overnight.*

6

Making an Insect Spreading Board

Materials

- WOODEN BASE
- 2 PIECES OF HEAVY CARDBOARD
- 8 THUMBTACKS
- 4 PINS
- 2 NARROW STRIPS OF PAPER

Carefully cut the cardboard the size of the wings of the insect. Use the thumbtacks to fasten the pieces of cardboard to the wooden base (Fig. 6-1). Position the cardboard pieces side by side, and separate them by a space the size of the body of the insect. Place the body in this space, and spread the wings over the cardboard. Use the strips of paper that are the size of the wings of the insect and the pins (Fig. 6-2) to hold the wings in place until they dry in an open position (Fig. 6-3).

Fig. 6-1. *Use thumbtacks to hold the cardboard in place.*

Fig. 6-2. *Use paper strips and pins to hold the wings in place.*

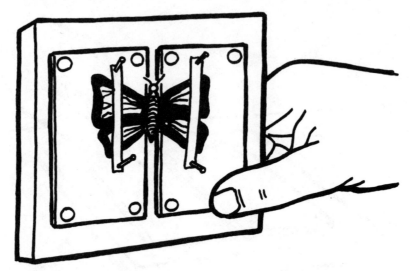

Fig. 6-3. *Let the insect dry with the wings in an open position.*

7

Mounting Insects

Materials
- DEAD INSECTS
- PINS
- CARDBOARD

Identify and record each insect (Fig. 7-1). Carefully push the pin through the middle body (thorax) of the dead insect (Fig. 7-2). The abdomen might not be firm enough to hold the insect in a lifelike position. Stick the pin upright in the cardboard base. This allows the underside, as well as the top, of the insect to be examined (Fig. 7-3).

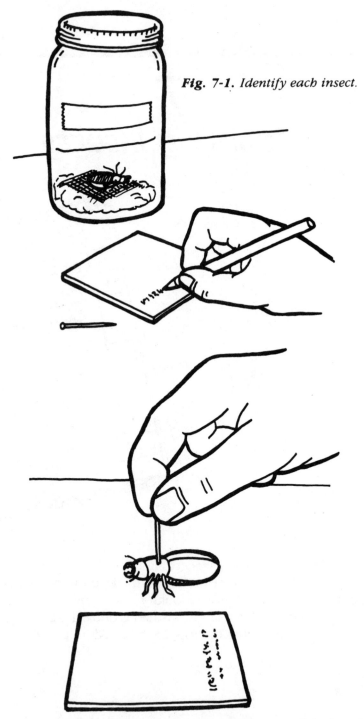

Fig. 7-1. *Identify each insect.*

Fig. 7-2. *Push the pin through the middle part of the insect.*

Fig. 7-3. *The top and the bottom of the insect can be examined.*

8

Starting an Ant Colony

Find a nest under logs or rocks. Notice the kind of food the ants are bringing in. You will have to provide their food. Some ants are meat eaters, while others feed largely on plants. Use the shovel and carefully cut around the nest in about a 16-inch circle (Fig. 8-1). Pry up this mound of dirt, and place it and the ants on the white cloth. Be careful when working with ants since some small insects can sting or bite. Examine the contents until you locate the queen (Fig. 8-2). She should be larger and shinier than the rest of the ants. You also should see ants who are scurrying around carrying whitish-colored ant pupae and shinier objects called *ant larvae*. The larvae are hatched from the eggs and shed their skins several times before they become pupae.

Fig. 8-1. *Use a shovel to dig out the nest.*

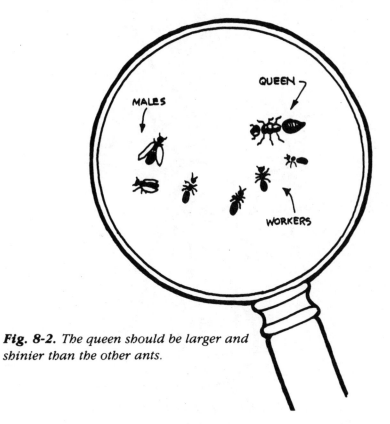

Fig. 8-2. *The queen should be larger and shinier than the other ants.*

Pupae are ants who are immobile and are in the nonfeeding transformation stage before becoming adults. Collect about three dozen of these pupae and larvae along with about the same number of adult ants. Collect the queen because she produces the eggs for the new generation. Fold the cloth into a bag and tie it with the string (Fig. 8-3). Take it home to transfer the ants and soil to the new nest.

Fig. 8-3. Collect the ants in the cloth bag.

Make sure the jars are clean and dry. Put the lid on the smaller jar, and place it inside the larger jar (Fig. 8-4). Try to keep the smaller jar in the center and fill the space between the two jars with the soil from the nest. A paper funnel can be used to transfer ants and soil (Fig. 8-5). Fill the space to within a couple of inches of the top. Punch a few holes in the lid to let in air. Cover the jar with the dark cloth for a couple of weeks to let the ants get settled and start to tunnel (Fig. 8-6). Remove the cover for observations. Keep a small piece of damp sponge in the nest for moisture (Fig. 8-7), and try to determine what kind of food your ants prefer.

Fig. 8-4. Place the smaller jar inside the larger one.

Fig. 8-5. *Use a paper funnel to transfer the ants and the soil.*

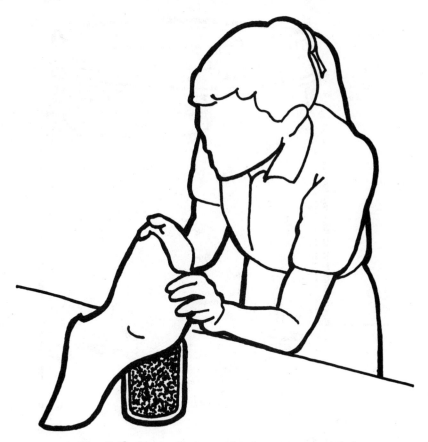

Fig. 8-6. *Cover the jar to let the ants get settled.*

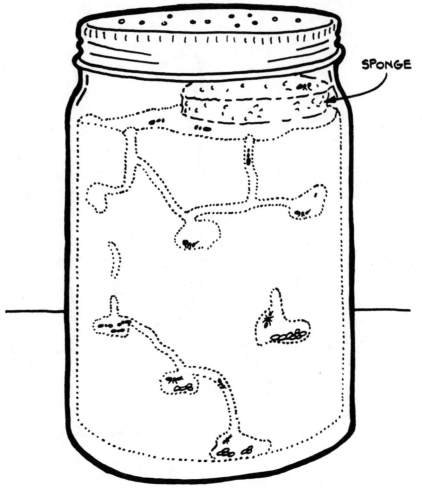

SPONGE

Fig. 8-7. *A damp sponge will keep moisture in the jar.*

9
From a Caterpillar to a Butterfly or Moth

Materials
- CATERPILLAR
- FRESH LEAVES
- WATER
- CAGE

Collect a few caterpillars and the leaves on which they are feeding (Fig. 9-1). Place them in the cage, and keep them supplied with fresh leaves (Fig. 9-2). When the caterpillar has finished growing, it will hang by its tail from a safe location under a board or leaf and build itself a protective cover (Fig. 9-3)—a cocoon for a moth and a chrysalis, the hard-shelled pupa, for a butterfly. The cage should be placed outside through the winter. In the spring, sprinkle the leaves with water, about once a week and the adults will emerge. Provide them with fresh leaves, and set them free when you have made your observations (Fig. 9-4).

Fig. 9-1. *Collect the caterpillars and the leaves they are feeding on.*

Fig. 9-2. *Keep the caterpillars supplied with fresh leaves.*

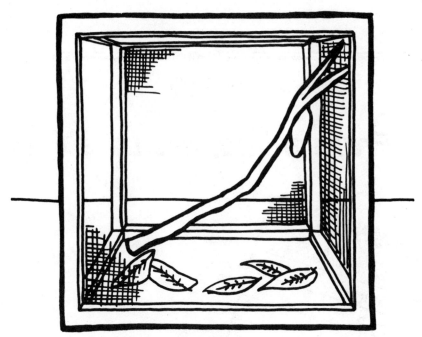

Fig. 9-3. *The caterpillar will build a cocoon.*

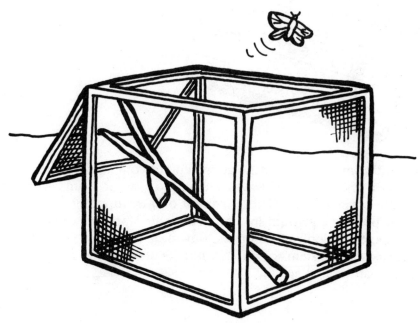

Fig. 9-4. *Set them free when you have finished your experiment.*

10
From a Tadpole to a Frog

Materials

- AQUARIUM
- WATER
- SAND
- A FEW TADPOLES
- WATER PLANTS
- ALGAE-COVERED ROCKS FROM NEARBY POND
- BITS OF HARD-BOILED EGG
- MAGNIFYING GLASS

Build a small beach of sand at one end of your aquarium (Fig. 10-1). Add a few inches of water, a couple of water plants, and a few algae-covered rocks. Drop in about 6 or 8 tadpoles (Fig. 10-2). Do not put the aquarium in direct sunlight. Warm water will kill the tadpoles. Tadpoles feed on the tiny algae that grow on underwater rocks and the stems of water plants. Older tadpoles can be fed bits of a hard-boiled egg.

Fig. 10-1. *Make a sandy beach at one end of your aquarium.*

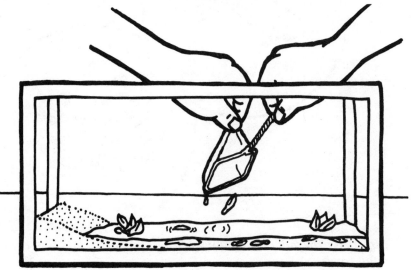

Fig. 10-2. *Place the tadpoles in the aquarium.*

Use the magnifying glass to monitor the changes as the tadpoles grow. The complete change can take a few months, or in the case of the bullfrog species, up to two years, but they will gradually grow legs, lose their tail, and turn into adult frogs (Fig. 10-3).

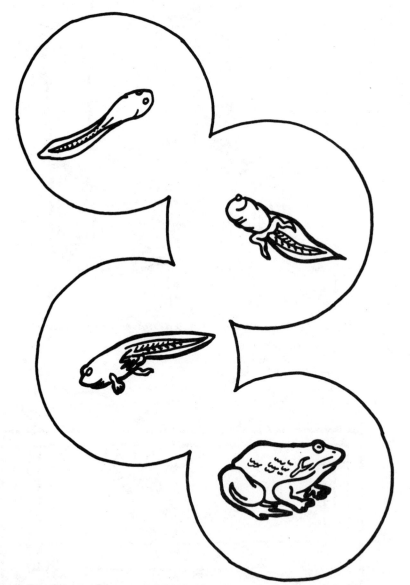

Fig. 10-3. *The tadpole will slowly grow legs, lose its tail, and become an adult frog.*

11

Frogs in Hibernation

Materials
- AQUARIUM
- WATER
- DIRT
- WIRE SCREEN
- FROG

Construct a semi-aquatic aquarium by building a mud bank leading up to a small hill of dirt at one end, and a small pool of water in the other end (Fig. 11-1). Try to make it a natural surrounding. Feed your frog live insects such as small bugs and flies. Notice the breathing of the frog. This can be seen in the rapid pulsing of its throat. In the fall of the year, place the aquarium outside in the cold for several hours (Fig. 11-2). Look at the frog's throat. You should see that its breathing has slowed, and the frog appears sluggish. It

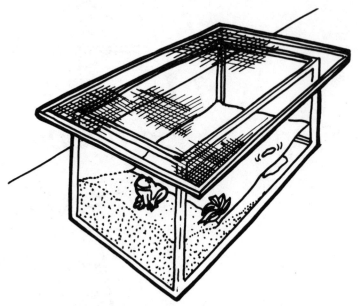

Fig. 11-1. *Have a small hill of dirt at one end of the aquarium and a small pool of water at the other end.*

Fig. 11-2. *When fall comes, place the aquarium outside in the cold for a few hours.*

will start to burrow into the mud bank and go into hibernation (Fig. 11-3). If you have mild winters, you might try scattering ice cubes inside the aquarium. This also can cause the frog to go into hibernation. At this time, frogs go into a long sleep until the warmth of spring wakes them up.

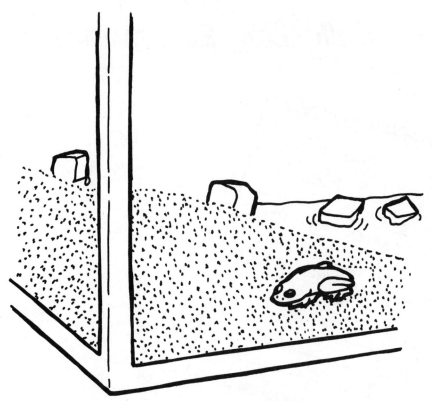

Fig. 11-3. *The frog will burrow into the dirt to hibernate.*

12
Collecting Earthworms

Materials

- COFFEE CAN
- SHOVEL
- GARDEN SOIL OR WARM, MOIST SOIL
- MAGNIFYING GLASS

Earthworms like to live in soil that is rich in humus and decaying plant or animal material. Push the shovel deep into this type of soil, and turn it upside down. This should uncover the worms. Fill the can with this dirt and add worms as you find them (Fig. 12-1). Earthworms also can be found on top of the ground and sidewalks after a rainstorm. They come to the surface to get air because the soaking rain water forces out the air in the soil. Examine the worms with the magnifying glass (Fig. 12-2). You will see that they have a long slender body that is covered with a slimy fluid. You also can see that the worm is divided into segments, or rings, and is reddish-brown in color. The earthworm has no eyes, but there is a pair of

Fig. 12-1. *Place the worms in the can of dirt.*

Fig. 12-2. *A close-up view of a worm.*

spots on each segment that is sensitive to light. Tiny bristles underneath and on each side of its body help the worm pull itself along by contracting its muscles (Fig. 12-3). Earthworms are some of the most important animals on earth. They keep the ground porous. This helps the growth of plants.

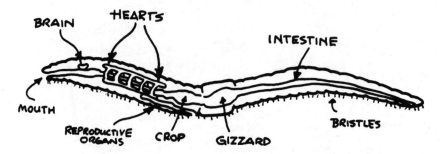

Fig. 12-3. Tiny bristles help the worm pull itself along.

13
Keeping Earthworms

Materials

- LARGE WIDE-MOUTH JAR, OR OLD AQUARIUM
- RICH SOIL
- LEAF MOLD
- SAND
- WATER
- VEGETABLE LEAVES
- CORNMEAL OR OATMEAL
- DARK CLOTH

Materials

- EARTHWORMS

Fill the jar with layers of sand, leaf mold, and soil. Sprinkle each layer with a little water as you fill the jar. Place a small handful of cornmeal or oatmeal on the top of the last layer, and add a few small pieces of a vegetable leaf (Fig. 13-1). Place several earthworms in the jar (Fig. 13-2), and cover it with the dark cloth (Fig. 13-3). Let it set for about a week. This will make the worms feel at home and encourage them to tunnel near the sides of the jar (Fig. 13-4). Keep the soil moist, and add food about twice a week.

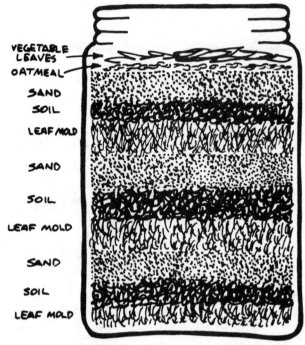

VEGETABLE
LEAVES
OATMEAL
SAND
SOIL
LEAF MOLD
SAND
SOIL
LEAF MOLD
SAND
SOIL
LEAF MOLD

Fig. 13-1. *Place a few small pieces of a vegetable leaf on top.*

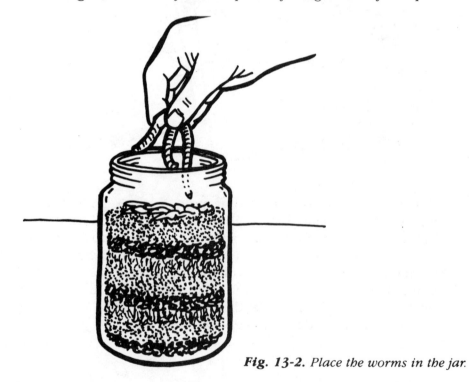

Fig. 13-2. *Place the worms in the jar.*

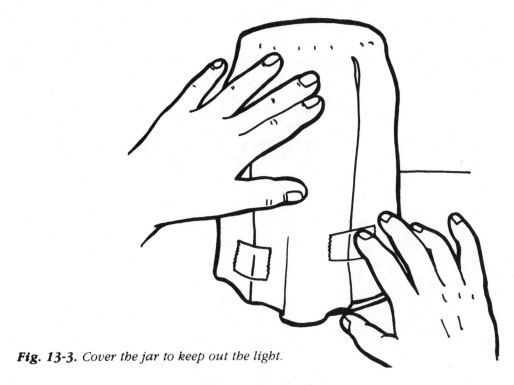

Fig. 13-3. *Cover the jar to keep out the light.*

Fig. 13-4. *The worms should tunnel near the sides of the jar.*

14

Keeping a Turtle

Materials

- TURTLE
- TERRARIUM
- COARSE SAND
- DIRT OR FINE SAND

It is against the law in some places to take turtles from the wild. Small turtles can often be found in pet stores. Your terrarium should be as close as possible to the natural habitat of the turtle you buy. This includes the temperature and humidity. You can use an old aquarium or make a terrarium from a cardboard or wooden box. Cut out one side of the box and glue in a transparent piece of plastic (Fig. 14-1). Water must be kept in a pan or bowl. It can be sunk in the soil to simulate a small pond. Pour a layer of coarse sand in the bottom of your terrarium. Add a layer of dirt, or fine sand, depending on the type of turtle you have (Fig. 14-2). Plants of that

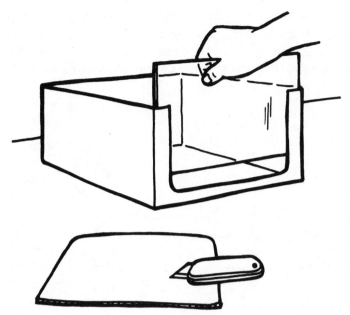

Fig. 14-1. *Glue a piece of plastic in one end.*

Fig. 14-2. *Add a layer of dirt or sand.*

habitat can be added (Fig. 14-3). Sprinkle the soil and plants with water, daily if the turtles are used to moisture, or only once a week if it is a desert terrarium. Some turtles will eat bits of fruit and vegetables. Others prefer insects and pieces of meat, such as liver.

Fig. 14-3. Add plants and fresh water to your terrarium.

15
Parts of a Fish

Look at Fig. 15-1 and notice the different parts of the fish's body. The fish was the first animal with a backbone, and they are in greater numbers than any other animal with a backbone. A fish breathes with gills instead of lungs. Gills contain blood vessels that absorb oxygen through the thin membranes in the gills. Fish take in oxygen and give off carbon dioxide. In place of arms and legs, they have two pairs of fins; the pectoral fins, just behind the head, operate like our arms, and the pelvic fins, located on the lower part of the body, correspond to our legs. The remaining fins serve as keels and rudders (Fig. 15-1). Fish are coldblooded and their body

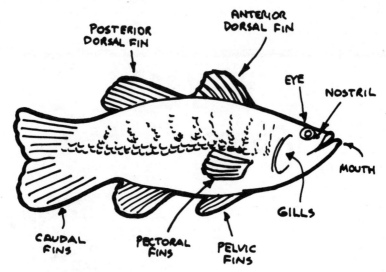

Fig. 15-1. Parts of a fish's body.

temperature is about the same as the water in which they live. Their internal organs (brain, nerves, skeleton, and muscles) are similar to other backboned animals (Fig. 15-2). Most fish, however, depend heavily on a sense of smell and a special sense in the lateral line. This is a row of tubes and pores over a nerve that runs along the side of the fish's body. This sense organ is able to detect the slightest of vibrations. There are many different kinds of fish who live in the oceans, lakes, and streams all over the world. Their size, shape, and the way they live depends on the particular place in which they live.

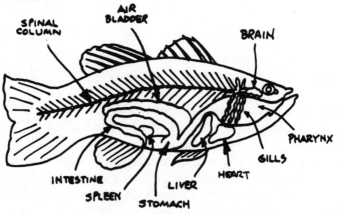

Fig. 15-2. An inside look at a fish.

16
Raising Guppies

Materials

- LARGE BOWL OR AN AQUARIUM
- WATER
- CLEAN SAND OR FINE GRAVEL
- WATER PLANTS
- GUPPIES
- HATCHING BOWL

Place a layer of sand in the bottom of the aquarium (Fig. 16-1), and add plants (Fig. 16-2), or other suitable objects, to provide hiding places for the young. The mother guppy will eat her young. Add water at the rate of one gallon for every pair of guppies. Guppies like warm water, between 70° and 100° Fahrenheit (Fig. 16-3). Feed your guppies commercial fish food such as brine shrimp, but be careful not to overfeed. It may take about a month for the new guppies to appear, but when the female is about to produce her young, separate

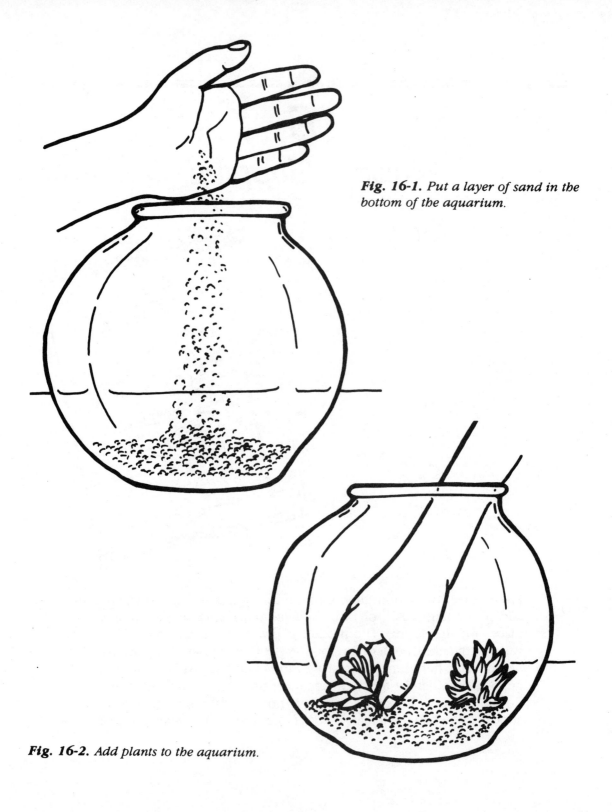

Fig. 16-1. *Put a layer of sand in the bottom of the aquarium.*

Fig. 16-2. *Add plants to the aquarium.*

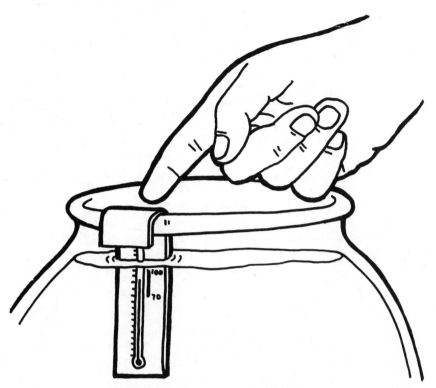

Fig. 16-3. *Guppies prefer warm water.*

her from the rest of the fish. Place her in a separate container (Fig. 16-4). As soon as the guppies are born, return the mother to the aquarium. Otherwise, she will quickly devour the young. When the young guppies get larger, place them in the aquarium with the rest of the fish.

Fig. 16-4. Separate the mother from the baby guppies.

17
Parts of a Bird

Look at the illustration and notice the different parts of a bird (Fig. 17-1). There are many different kinds of birds, and they vary in size and shape. But all their bodies are similar. The skeleton of a bird is specifically designed for flying. The bones are thin and small, but they still do their job. The longer bones are hollow to keep down weight (Fig. 17-2). The bones fit together in such a way that makes the skeleton a rigid framework except for the neck. It is flexible and allows the bird to reach any part of its body with its beak. A little sparrow has twice as many bones in its neck as a giraffe. More than half of the bird's weight is made up of muscles. The largest

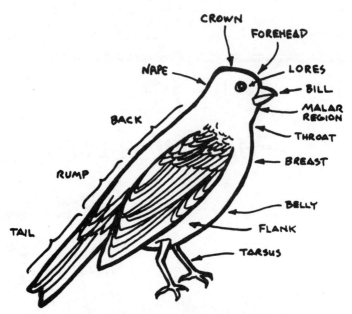

Fig. 17-1. *Different parts of a bird.*

Fig. 17-2. *Birds have hollow bones to keep down weight.*

are the muscles in its breast that operate the wings. Feathers give the bird the ability to fly (Fig. 17-3). They streamline its body and maintain the body temperature. The larger feathers on the tip of the wing are the primary feathers. They are connected to bones that correspond to our hands. The secondary feathers, closer in to the body, are connected to bones that correspond to our forearms. These feathers open as the bird pulls its wings up and forward, then close when it pushes down and back against the air. Birds have excellent eyesight and hearing, but their sense of smell and taste are not as good. It is believed that the ancestors of birds were reptiles, because they have many of the same characteristics as reptiles (Fig. 17-4).

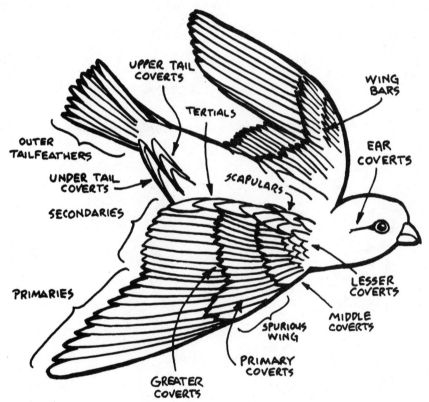

Fig. 17-3. Feathers allow birds to fly.

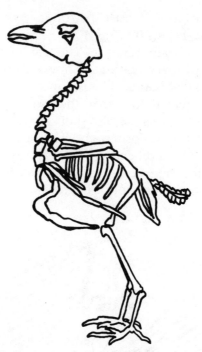

Fig. 17-4. *The ancestors of birds might have been reptiles.*

18

Studying and Identifying Birds

Materials
- NOTEBOOK AND PENCIL
- POCKET-SIZED BIRD IDENTIFICATION BOOK
- BINOCULARS

Study pictures of birds and try to learn their names (Fig. 18-1). Look for birds in their natural surroundings such as trees, underbrush, and near water (Fig. 18-2). City parks can be a good place to start. It also helps to go with someone who already knows about birds. Zoos have live birds from other countries, and museums often have exhibits of stuffed birds in lifelike surroundings.

Birds are easily frightened, so it is important to move slowly and quietly. Dull-colored clothes will help keep you from being noticeable in woods or fields. You can hide near a nest, and wait for the birds to come and go. Birdbaths are good places to observe

Fig. 18-1. *Learn to identify birds in your area.*

Fig. 18-2. *Birds can be found in trees and bushes.*

birds who are drinking and bathing. First, notice the size and shape of the bird (Fig. 18-3). Look for colors and the patterns of the feathers (Fig. 18-4). Listen for their songs or calls, and notice the pattern of their flights (Fig. 18-5). Some birds soar, while others fly in jerky up and down flights. It will be easy to tell a sparrow from a robin, and in time, you will be able to identify many other varieties (Fig. 18-6).

Fig. 18-3. Notice the body of the bird; its size and shape.

Fig. 18-4. Notice the color and patterns of the feathers.

Fig. 18-5. *Humming birds can hover then dart off in any direction.*

Fig. 18-6. *Soon you will be able to identify the birds in your area.*

19
Building a Bird House

Materials

- OLD UNPAINTED WOOD
- DRILL
- HAMMER AND NAILS
- SAW
- NESTING MATERIAL

The size and shape of the house depends on the type of bird. But weathered, unpainted wood is preferred over metal. Roofs should be sloped to allow the rain to run off. You might even drill a couple of small holes in the floor to let out any rainwater that might get in. A few holes that are drilled in the walls, just under the roof overhang, will provide ventilation and help in cooling the inside (Fig. 19-1). Generally, the floor of the house should be about 5 × 5 inches, and walls about 8 to 10 inches high (Fig. 19-2). The hole for the entrance should be about 2 inches in diameter and in the upper half of the front wall (Fig. 19-3). The bird house can be mounted on a post or fastened to a tree, and should be from 6 to 15 feet above

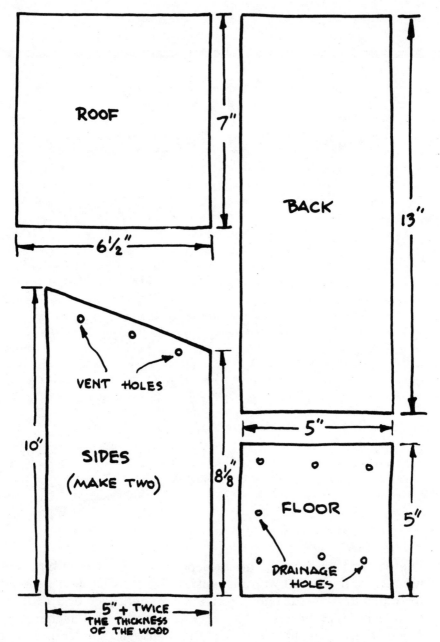

Fig. 19-1. *A pattern for a typical bird house.*

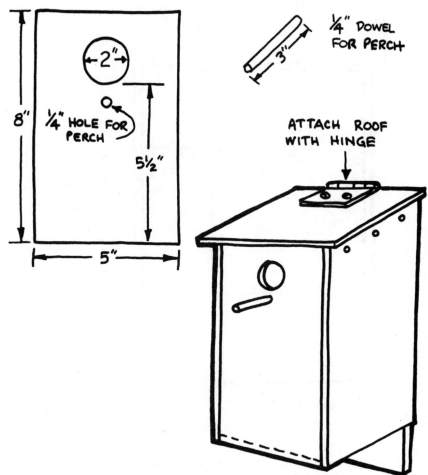

FRONT:

2"

8"

¼" HOLE FOR PERCH

5½"

5"

¼" DOWEL FOR PERCH

3"

ATTACH ROOF WITH HINGE

Fig. 19-2. A bird house with a hinged roof.

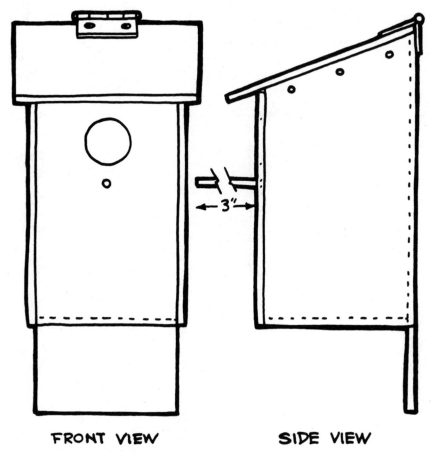

FRONT VIEW   **SIDE VIEW**

Fig. 19-3. Front and side view of a bird house.

the ground. Place a sheet of tin around the post or tree trunk to protect the birds from cats and squirrels. Early in the spring, place nesting material that can include yarn, pieces of rag, twigs, and bits of wood shavings on the ground close to the bird house. The nesting birds will find it and use what they need. Use the illustrations for a reference and notice that a robin likes an open nesting shelf (Fig. 19-4), while purple martins prefer apartment living (Fig. 19-5).

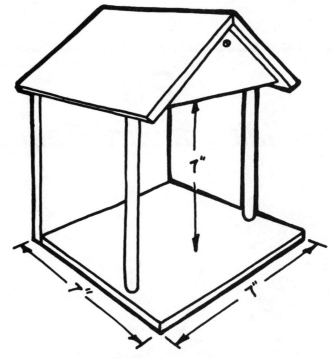

ROBIN HOUSE
Fig. 19-4. Robins like an open house.

PURPLE MARTIN HOUSE
Fig. 19-5. Purple martins prefer apartments.

20
Building a Bird Feeder

Materials

- UNPAINTED WOOD
- HAMMER AND NAILS
- SAW

A feeding tray is easy to make. All you need is a board about 12 inches long and about 12 inches wide. Add strips of wood around the edges to keep the food from falling off, and place it near a window (Fig. 20-1). Make sure the tray is out of reach of cats and other enemies of birds. A metal fence guard will discourage hungry cats (Fig. 20-2). You also can build a trolley feeder. Run a small rope, like a clothesline, from a window to a tree or post. Attach straps and pulleys to a feeding tray and use a string to pull it closer to the window as the birds lose their shyness (Fig. 20-3). You can add a

Fig. 20-1. *Place the feeding tray near a window.*

roof to your feeding tray to keep out the rain and snow (Fig. 20-4). A couple of holes that are drilled in the floor will let rain and snow drain out.

You can feed birds suet, or beef fat, and scraps of meat. Many birds like grains, bread crumbs, and crumpled dog biscuits. You also can use boiled potatoes, finely chopped hard-boiled eggs, raw or boiled rice, and fruits. Just remember that if you give the birds too much food, they will become dependent on you and lose their self-reliance. If this happens, they will not forage for themselves, and in winter, if you're not there to feed them, they could freeze and die.

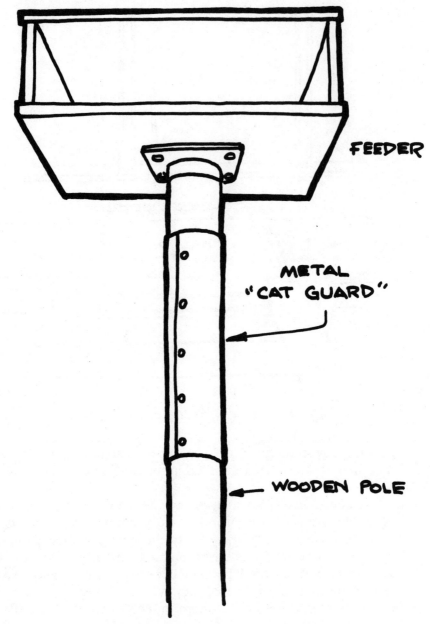

FEEDER

METAL "CAT GUARD"

WOODEN POLE

Fig. 20-2. *Metal guards keep cats away.*

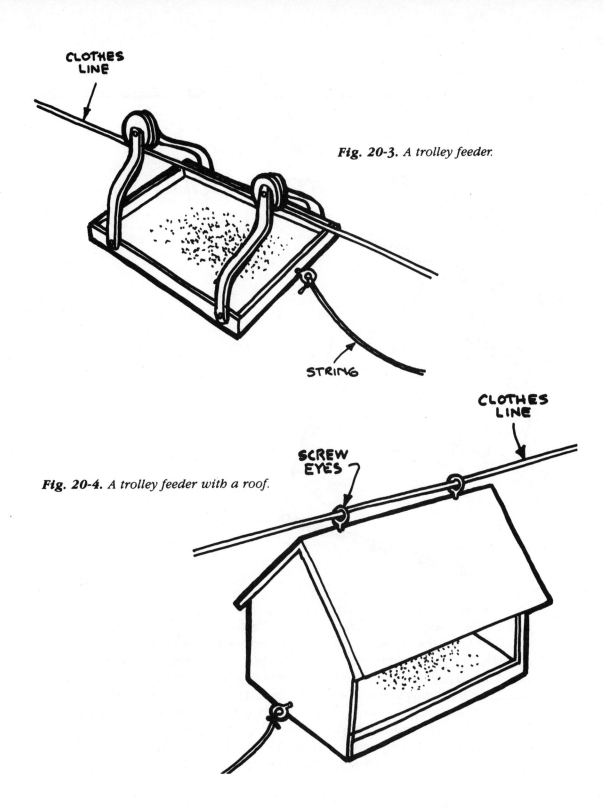

Fig. 20-3. *A trolley feeder.*

CLOTHES LINE

STRING

Fig. 20-4. *A trolley feeder with a roof.*

SCREW EYES

CLOTHES LINE

21

The Human Body

Materials

OBSERVATION

The human body can be thought of as containing seven systems: (1) the skeleton, or skeletal system is the framework of bones (Fig. 21-1); (2) the muscular system supports and moves the skeleton (Fig. 21-2); (3) digestive system supplies the blood with digested food to provide the body with energy (Fig. 21-3); (4) the circulatory system extends throughout the body sending blood that is carrying food and oxygen, and on the return trip, carries away nitrogen wastes and carbon dioxide (Fig. 21-4); (5) the urinary system removes nitrogen wastes from the blood (Fig. 21-5); (6) the respiratory system allows us to take in oxygen from the air and

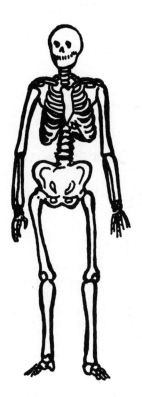

Fig. 21-1. The human skeleton.

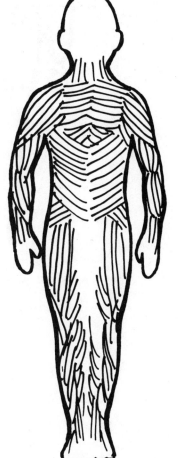

MUSCLES,
TENDONS,
& LIGAMENTS

Fig. 21-2. Muscles support the skeleton
and make it move.

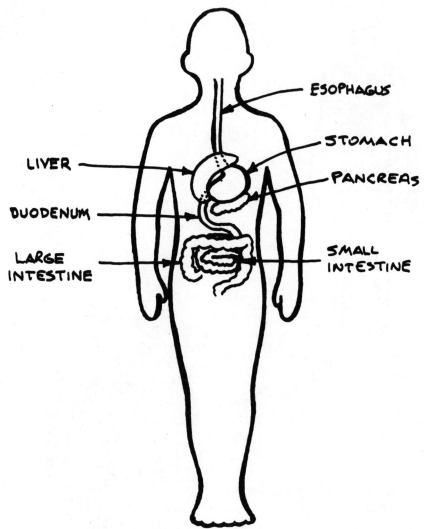

Fig. 21-3. *The human digestive system.*

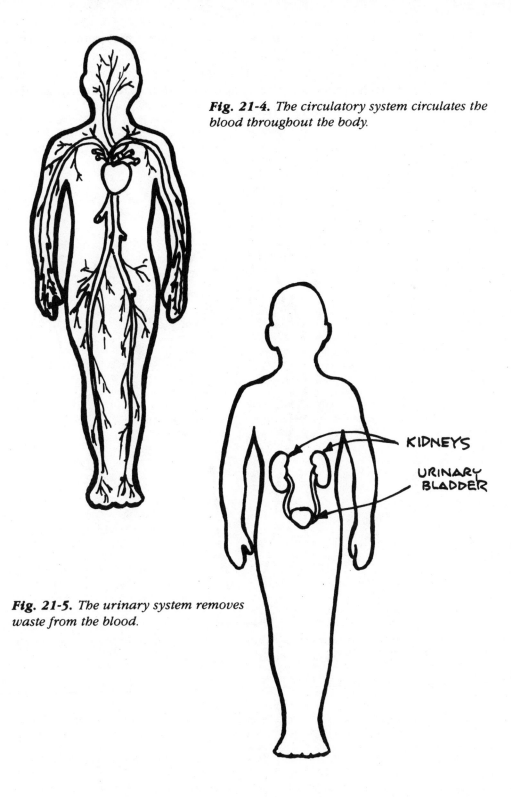

Fig. 21-4. *The circulatory system circulates the blood throughout the body.*

KIDNEYS

URINARY BLADDER

Fig. 21-5. *The urinary system removes waste from the blood.*

deliver it to our blood, and at the same time, remove carbon dioxide from the blood and release it back into the air (Fig. 21-6); and (7) the nervous system is the system that carries messages between the brain and the organs and other parts of the body (Fig. 21-7).

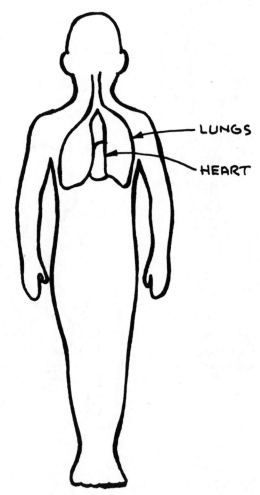

Fig. 21-6. *The respiratory system lets us take in oxygen and remove carbon dioxide from our blood.*

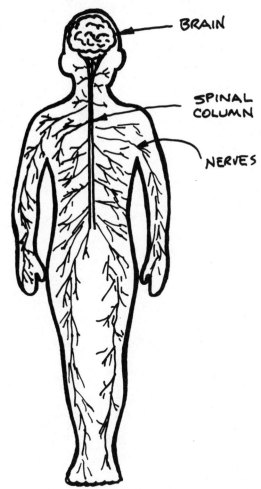

BRAIN

SPINAL
COLUMN

NERVES

Fig. 21-7. *The nervous system carries messages from the brain to all parts of the body.*

PART VI

PLANT BIOLOGY

1

How Plants Prevent Erosion

Soften the ground around the plant with water (Fig. 1-1). Then grab the plant around the stem, near the ground, and carefully pull it from the dirt (Fig. 1-2). Examine the roots (Fig. 1-3). You should see the roots still clinging to a small amount of soil (Fig. 1-4).

Running water is the greatest cause of erosion. Roots from plants grow down through the dirt and hold the soil together (Fig. 1-5). This helps prevent the soil from being washed away.

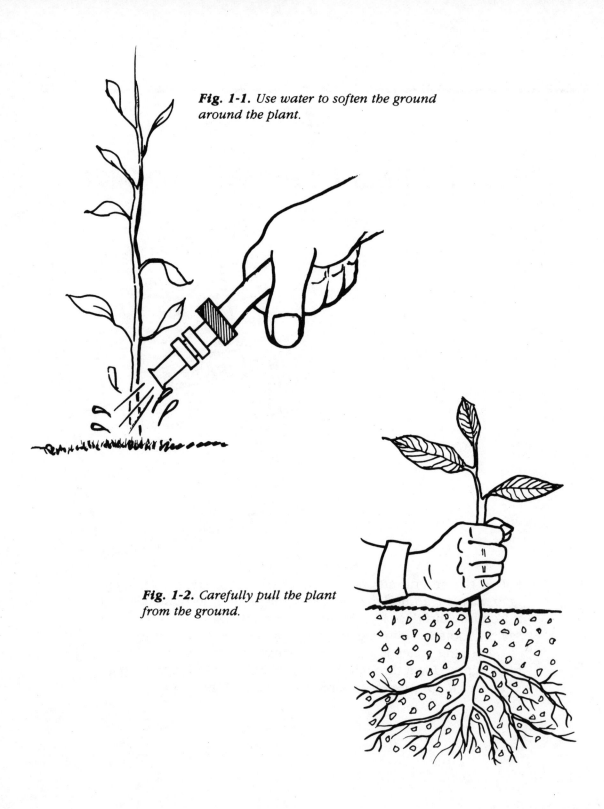

Fig. 1-1. Use water to soften the ground around the plant.

Fig. 1-2. Carefully pull the plant from the ground.

Fig. 1-3. Look closely at the roots.

Fig. 1-4. The roots will be holding a small mass of soil.

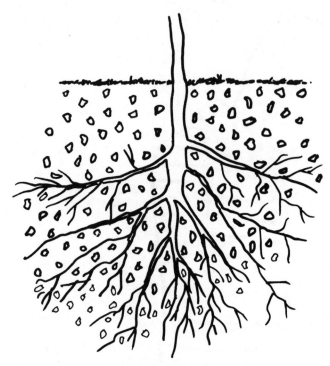

Fig. 1-5. *The roots of plants help hold the soil together to prevent erosion.*

2

Why Plants Have Roots

Materials

- FRESH STALK OF CELERY WITH LEAVES
- LARGE BOWL
- JAR
- KNIFE
- RED FOOD COLORING
- WATER
- TWEEZERS

Fill the jar about half full of water and add a few drops of food coloring (Fig. 2-1). Fill the bowl about half full of water. Now place the lower end of the celery in the bowl and, keeping it under water, cut about an inch from the bottom of the stalk. Now place the stalk in the jar of red water and let it stand until the leaves are colored red (Fig. 2-2).

Examine the celery and notice the red color in the stalk and the leaves. Cut across the stem and you will see the tubes that carry the water (Fig. 2-3). You can even separate the stem with tweezers and follow the red streaks up to the leaves. This is the path the water takes when the plant is growing in the ground.

The roots take in water and dissolved minerals, not through the part of the root that has a tough, thick covering, but through the tiny white thread-like parts called root hairs. Water and dissolved minerals pass through the thin walls of the root hairs, up through the roots, then through the tubes to the leaves. This is how plants get their food.

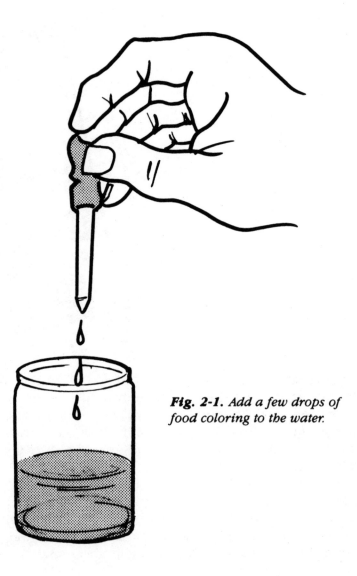

Fig. 2-1. *Add a few drops of food coloring to the water.*

Fig. 2-2. *Place the stalk in the colored water and let it stand.*

Fig. 2-3. *Tubes carry the water through the stalk to the leaves.*

3

Why Plants Have Leaves

Materials

- POTTED PLANT
- THIN CARDBOARD OR PAPER
- PAPER CLIP
- SCISSORS

Cut two pieces of cardboard the same size. Each side should be 1 inch long (Fig. 3-1). Place one piece on top and one on the bottom of a leaf near the top of the plant (Fig. 3-2). Fasten the pieces in place with the paper clip (Fig. 3-3). Next, place the plant in a sunny location for a few days (Fig. 3-4). Now remove the paper clip and the pieces of cardboard. Examine the leaf and notice the area that did not get sunlight.

You should see that this area is a lighter color (Fig. 3-5). This is because the plant was unable to produce *chlorophyll* in the area covered by the pieces of cardboard. The word chlorophyll comes from two Greek words, meaning light-green leaf. Chlorophyll is in the form of tiny green specks grouped against the inside walls of the cells in the leaf. They give the leaf its green color.

Green plants must have carbon dioxide, water, minerals, and chlorophyll to make food. To do this, they must have light. The green leaves change light energy into chemical energy and the chemical energy is used to make food. This process is called *photosynthesis*. Photo means light and synthesis means putting together. So the term means putting together by light.

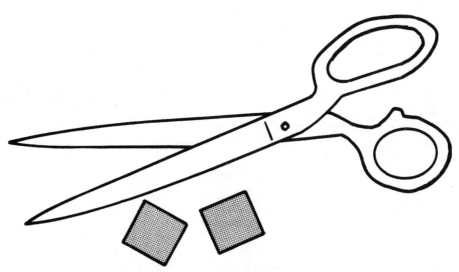

Fig. 3-1. *Cut two pieces of cardboard. Each side should be 1 inch long.*

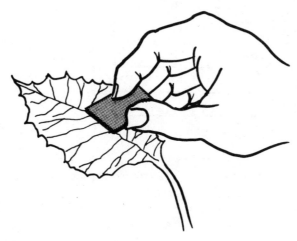

Fig. 3-2. *Place one on top and one on the bottom of a leaf.*

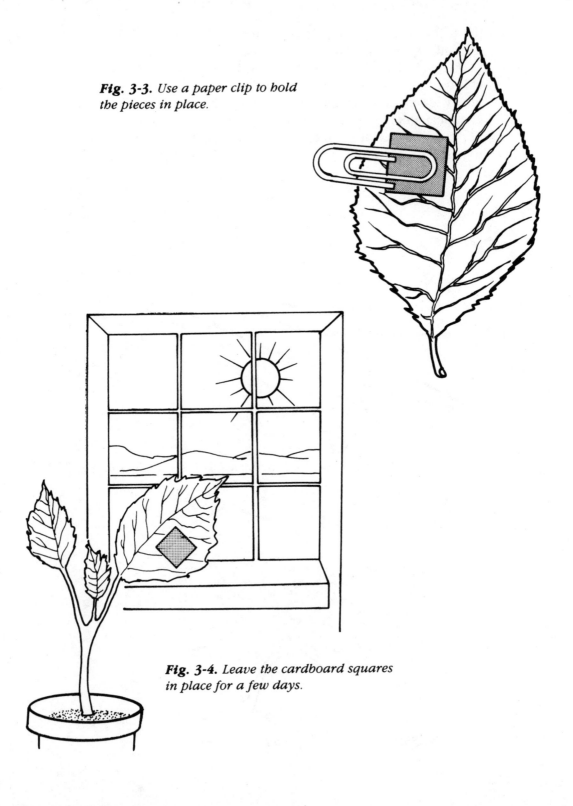

Fig. 3-3. Use a paper clip to hold the pieces in place.

Fig. 3-4. Leave the cardboard squares in place for a few days.

Fig. 3-5. _The area under the cardboard is a lighter color._

4

How Plants Breathe

Materials

- GROWING PLANT WITH LEAVES
- PETROLEUM JELLY

Apply a thin coat of petroleum jelly to the bottom surface of one of the leaves (Fig. 4-1). Next, apply a thin coat to the top surface of a nearby leaf (Fig. 4-2). Leave the coatings in place for a day or two. Now examine both leaves (Fig. 4-3). You will see that the leaf with the petroleum jelly on the bottom surface will be dying.

Tiny air holes, called *stomata*, so small they can only be seen through a microscope, are on the underside of the leaf. Stomata means little mouths. These holes are valves that open and close to bring in air and to give off water (Fig. 4-4). One of these valves is called a stoma. They usually open in daylight and close in darkness. There are many thousands to a square inch of leaf surface. The petroleum jelly sealed the holes so that the leaf couldn't breathe and started to die. Some leaves, however, have their stomata in their upper surfaces. The water lily, for example, must have its air holes in the upper surface because the lower surface is always in water.

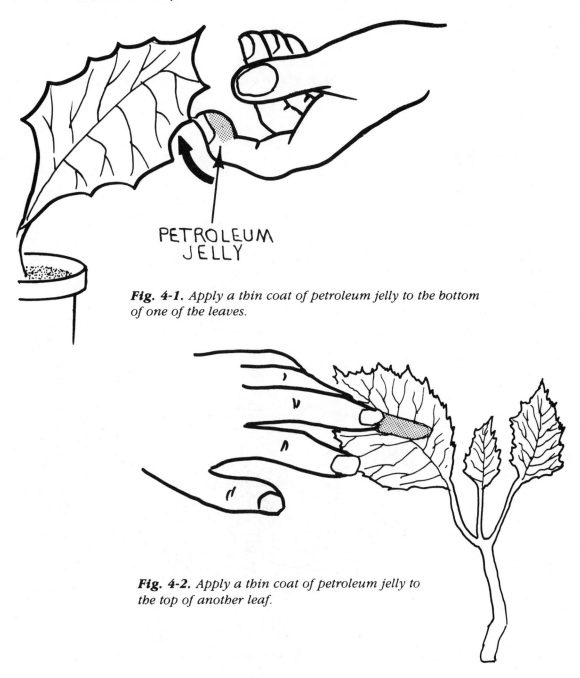

PETROLEUM JELLY

Fig. 4-1. Apply a thin coat of petroleum jelly to the bottom of one of the leaves.

Fig. 4-2. Apply a thin coat of petroleum jelly to the top of another leaf.

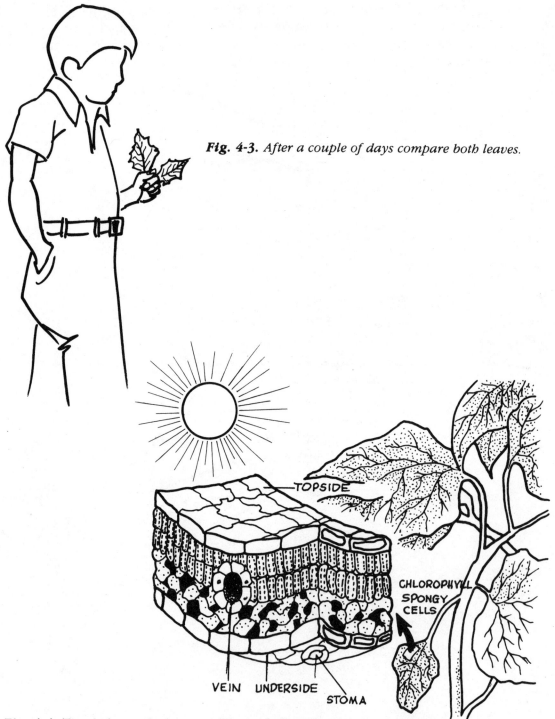

Fig. 4-3. *After a couple of days compare both leaves.*

TOPSIDE

CHLOROPHYLL
SPONGY
CELLS

VEIN   UNDERSIDE

STOMA

Fig. 4-4. *Tiny holes on the bottom of the leaf allow the plant to breathe.*

5

Why Plants Need Sunlight

Materials

2 BEAN PLANTS
ABOUT THE
SAME SIZE IN
SEPARATE POTS

Place one of the plants in normal sunlight (Fig. 5-1) and the other in a closet or someplace where no sunlight can get to it (Fig. 5-2). Water each plant as you normally would to keep them growing. Then, after a couple of weeks, remove the plant from the closet and place it next to the one in normal sunlight.

Notice the difference in their color (Fig. 5-3). The one from the closet should have lost most of its green color. This is because it did not receive any sunlight. The plant needs sunlight for the production of food by *photosynthesis*. The energy from sunlight is changed into food.

Some plants, such as mushrooms, have no chlorophyll and grow in dark places (Fig. 5-4). They do not make food like green leaf plants. They use food that has been produced by green leaf plants.

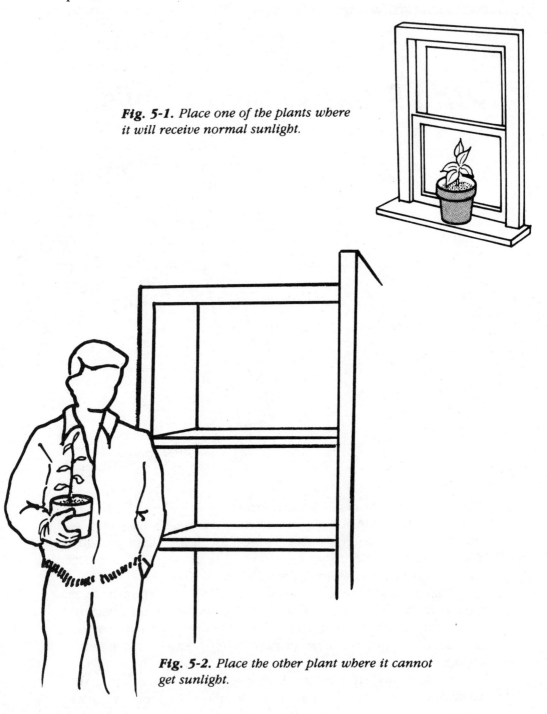

Fig. 5-1. *Place one of the plants where it will receive normal sunlight.*

Fig. 5-2. *Place the other plant where it cannot get sunlight.*

Fig. 5-3. Compare the color of the two plants.

Fig. 5-4. Mushrooms grow in dark places.

6

How Plants Respond to Light

Materials

- SMALL POTTED PLANT (GERANIUM LILY, ETC.)

Place the plant in a sunny window and notice the position of the leaves (Fig. 6-1). Keep the plant there for several days and watch the way the leaves grow (Fig. 6-2). Now turn the plant around so that the other side faces the window (Fig. 6-3). A few days later, notice the change in the position of the leaves.

Plants respond to activity around them. The leaves of some plants fold together and droop when the plant is touched or shaken. The leaves of tulips close at night and open in the morning, and sunflowers turn toward the sun. The roots of plants respond to gravity by growing down. The stems and leaves of plants respond to the light by growing upward.

Fig. 6-1. Place the plant in a sunny place.

Fig. 6-2. Notice that the leaves grow toward the sun.

Fig. 6-3. Turn the plant around and the other side will grow toward the sun.

7

How Leaves Give Off Moisture

Materials

- A THICK LEAF WITH A LONG STEM
- 2 GLASSES
- PIECE OF THIN CARDBOARD
- MODELING CLAY
- WATER
- PENCIL

Make a small hole in the center of the cardboard with the point of the pencil (Fig. 7-1). Push the leaf stem through the hole until the leaf almost rests on the cardboard (Fig. 7-2). The stem should continue several inches below the cardboard. Now press small pieces of clay against the cardboard and around the stem to seal the hole. This will prevent moisture from coming through. Fill one of the glasses with water and place the card on top of the glass (Fig. 7-3). The cardboard, with the leaf on top, should completely cover the top of the glass, and the stem should be in the water. Now put the empty glass upside down over the cardboard and cover the leaf (Fig. 7-4). Place the glasses in normal sunlight for a few hours.

Small drops of moisture will begin to appear on the inside of the top glass (Fig. 7-5).

The leaf gives off water that it has drawn up through its stem. This process is called *transpiration*. It is similar to *perspiration*, the production of sweat in animals. Plants give off water mostly through tiny openings (stomata) on the surface of the leaves. The amount of water they give off depends mostly on how much was soaked up by the roots of the plant.

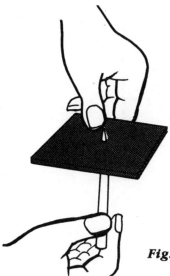

Fig. 7-1. *Make a small hole in the cardboard.*

Fig. 7-2. *Push the stem through the hole in the cardboard.*

Fig. 7-3. *Place the card on top of a glass of water.*

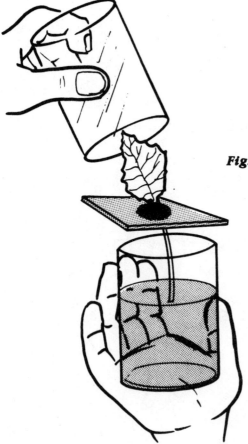

Fig. 7-4. *Place the empty glass over the leaf.*

Fig. **7-5.** *Moisture will form inside the empty glass.*

8
Why Leaves Fall

Materials

- BROAD TREE LEAVES (MAPLE, OAK OR ASH) IN AUTUMN AFTER THEY HAVE FALLEN

Look closely at one of the fallen leaves (Fig. 8-1). You will see that it has two main parts: the blade, and the stem, or *petiole* (Fig. 8-2). The blade is the broad part of the leaf that holds the green food-making cells. The stem holds the leaf to the plant, but it also brings water to the leaf and carries liquid food back from the leaf to all parts of the plant (Fig. 8-3).

During the summer, when the leaf is fully grown, it is producing large amounts of food. As summer continues, the young leaf begins to turn from a bright green to a darker blue-green.

Then something strange begins to happen in the base of the stem. A ring of cells, called *incision cells*, begins to turn into cork (Fig. 8-4). In late summer and early fall, these corky cells grow across the stem and slowly block the tiny tubes that carry water and food to and from the blade. By early October, the water supply is completely cut off and the leaf stops making food. With its food supply cut off, the leaf loses its green color and reveals its hidden colors of yellow, red, and orange or purple. The leaf continues to hang on until the stem breaks off cleanly through the incision (cork) cells and flutters to the ground (Fig. 8-5).

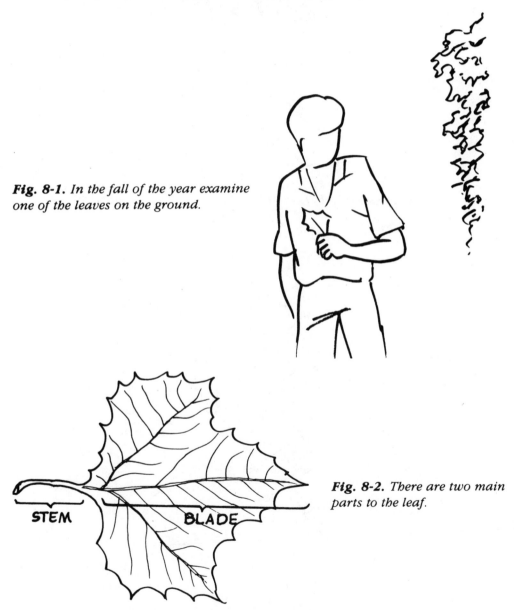

Fig. 8-1. In the fall of the year examine one of the leaves on the ground.

STEM   BLADE

Fig. 8-2. There are two main parts to the leaf.

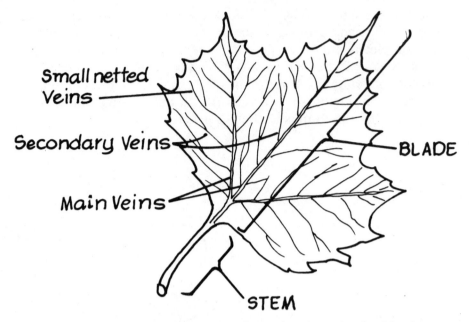

Fig. 8-3. *The stem takes water to the leaf and carries food back.*

Small netted Veins

Secondary Veins

Main Veins

BLADE

STEM

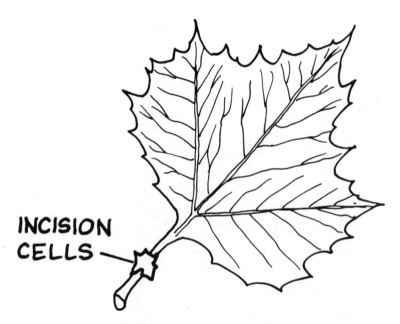

INCISION CELLS

Fig. 8-4. *In late summer incision cells turn into cork.*

Fig. 8-5. *The stem breaks clearly through the incision cells and the leaf falls to the ground.*

================= **Experiment** =================

9
How to Preserve Leaves

Materials

- FULL-GROWN LEAF
- NEWS PAPERS
- HEAVY BOOKS (FOR WEIGHT)
- THIN CARDBOARD SQUARE OR RECTANGLE
- GLUE
- SHELLAC

Place the leaf flat between several layers of newspaper (Fig. 9-1) and put books on top of the papers for weight (Fig. 9-2). After one day, some moisture (wetness) from the leaf will be absorbed by the papers. Replace the wet papers with dry ones. After about three days, the leaf should be dried and pressed. Now glue the leaf to the cardboard (Fig. 9-3) and apply shellac to the entire surface (Fig. 9-4). When the shellac dries, your leaf will be preserved for your collection.

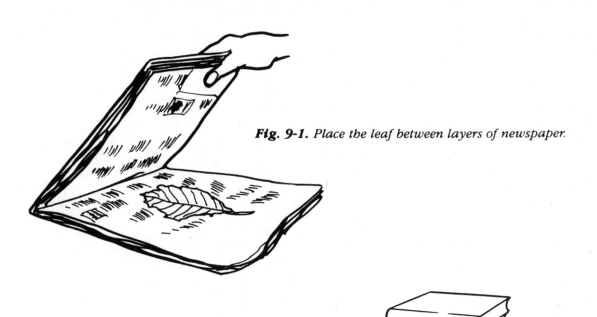

Fig. 9-1. Place the leaf between layers of newspaper.

Fig. 9-2. Use books to apply pressure to the papers.

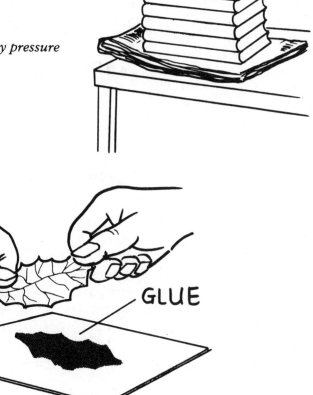

GLUE

Fig. 9-3. Glue the leaf to the cardboard.

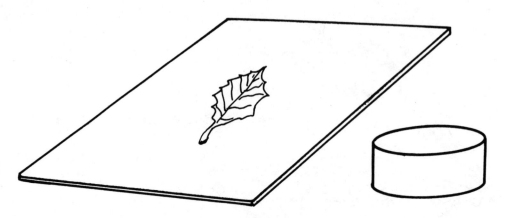

Fig. 9-4. Apply shellac to the surface and your leaf will be preserved.

10

Looking at the Age of a Tree

Look closely at the rings in the trunk (Fig. 10-1). These rings will tell you the tree's life story. Begin from the center and count a light and dark band as one year (Fig. 10-2). The center ring is the tree's first year of growth. The dark ring shows the growth in summer and the light band shows the growth in spring.

As you count outward from the center, the rings might be close together, showing that the tree grew slower because it was probably shaded from sunlight by other trees (Fig. 10-3). If the surrounding trees were cut down, the bands would be wider, showing that the growth speeded up. As a tree begins to reach its full size, the growth slows again and the bands become narrower.

Weather also affects the growth. During dry years the bands will be narrow, showing that the tree grew slower.

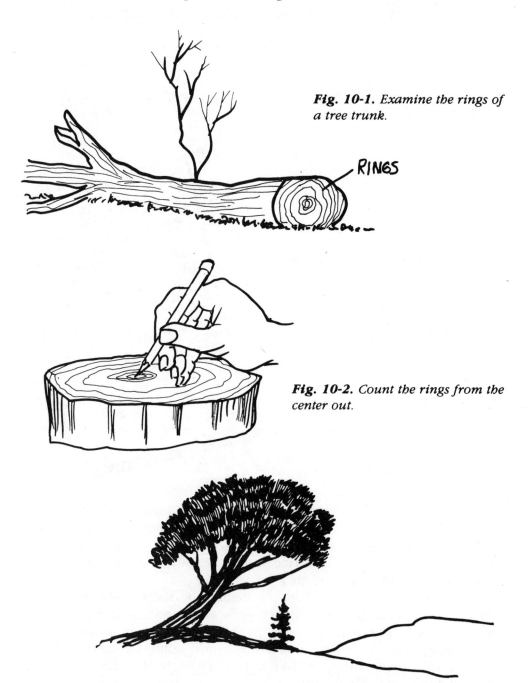

Fig. 10-1. *Examine the rings of a tree trunk.*

RINGS

Fig. 10-2. *Count the rings from the center out.*

Fig. 10-3. *Trees grow slower when they're shaded by larger trees.*

11
How Some Plants Produce New Shoots

Select a fairly long runner of an ivy plant. Beware of poison ivy! Bend the runner down to the ground (Fig. 11-1). Cover this section of the runner with damp soil (Fig. 11-2) and eventually it will root and grow a new plant. After the new roots have developed, the new plant can be cut from the parent stem. This method of producing new plants is called *layering*. Many plants reproduce this way naturally.

Fig. 11-1. *Bend a long ivy runner to the ground.*

Fig. 11-2. *Cover a section of the runner with damp soil.*

12
How to Grow a New
Plant from a Leaf

Break a leaf, with its stem, from the parent plant (Fig. 12-1) and plant it in the pot with about half of the stem covered by soil (Fig. 12-2). Keep the plant at room temperature. Water with liquid plant food every 14 days. High humidity (wetness in the air) is important. A plastic bag can be placed over the leaf to hold in moisture (Fig. 12-3). In a month, the leaf will have grown roots. In another 8 to 14 days, a new plant will appear, and in about 8 months, you should have a new adult plant.

Fig. 12-1. *Break a leaf and stem from the parent plant.*

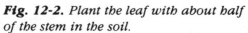

Fig. 12-2. *Plant the leaf with about half of the stem in the soil.*

Fig. 12-3. *A plastic bag will help hold in the moisture.*

13

A Look at Seeds

Materials

- A FEW MEDIUM OR LARGE DRIED BEANS OR PEAS
- MAGNIFYING GLASS
- BOWL
- WATER

Put the seeds in the bowl (Fig. 13-1) and cover them with water. Let them soak overnight. The next day, examine them closely and find a place on the seed where you can spread them open with your thumbnails (Fig. 13-2). After you have separated the seed, look at the inside of each of the two halves.

Notice the outer covering of the seed. This is the seed coat (Fig. 13-3). Inside the seed coat is a large area known as the "seed leaves," or *cotyledons* (Fig. 13-4). This is the food supply for the young plant that will grow from the seed. Now use the magnifying glass and look for the young plant. You should find a tiny pair of leaves (Fig. 13-5). You also might see the part that will become the root and stem of the future plant (Fig. 13-6). All plants, even the mighty tree, have such a small beginning.

Fig. 13-1. *Place a few bean seeds in a bowl and cover them with water.*

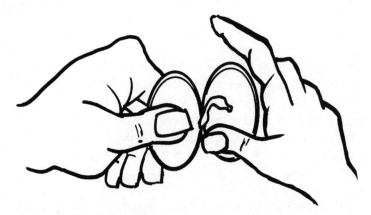

Fig. 13-2. *Use your thumbs to separate the seeds.*

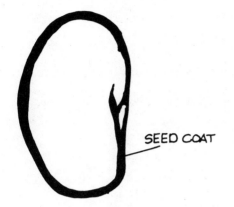

SEED COAT

Fig. 13-3. *The outer covering is the seed coat.*

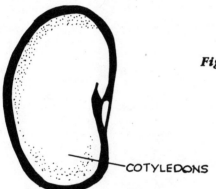

COTYLEDONS

Fig. 13-4. *The food supply is called the cotyledons.*

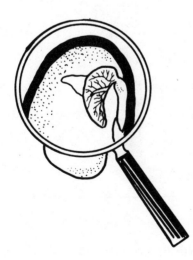

Fig. 13-5. *The tiny leaves of the young plant.*

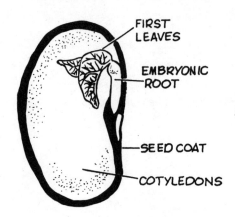

FIRST
LEAVES

EMBRYONIC
ROOT

SEED COAT

COTYLEDONS

Fig. 13-6. Inside view of bean seed.

14

How a Bean Grows

Fold the first paper towel into a strip about 4 inches wide (Fig. 14-1) and line the inside of the glass with it. Wad the other paper towel into a ball and place it in the circle formed by the first paper towel (Fig. 14-2). Now place the bean between the side of the glass and the paper towels, about an inch from the bottom of the glass (Fig. 14-3). You should have a clear side view of the bean. Next, pour water into the glass until the paper towels are completely wet (Fig. 14-4). Set the glass in a warm sunny place and you will see how a bean grows.

A few days after a seed has been planted, the young stem breaks out of the seed and begins to grow downward. It will form the main root and then the smaller roots (Fig. 14-5). While this is happening, the upper part of the stem quickly grows upward toward the sunlight, taking the seed and the food supply (the cotyledons) with it. Then the plant breaks through to the surface (Fig. 14-6). Now the cotyledons form the first leaves to appear above the surface (Fig. 14-7). They will store the food for the new plant (Fig. 14-8). The real leaves of the plant will grow from the tiny plant inside (Fig. 14-9). Within a couple of months, the plant will be producing bean seeds of its own.

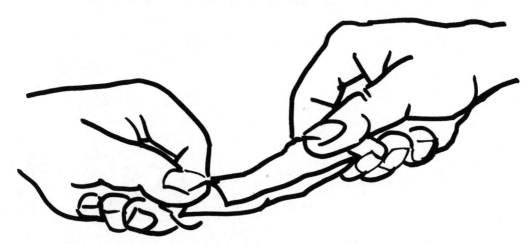

Fig. 14-1. *Fold the first paper towel into a strip and place it around the inside of the glass.*

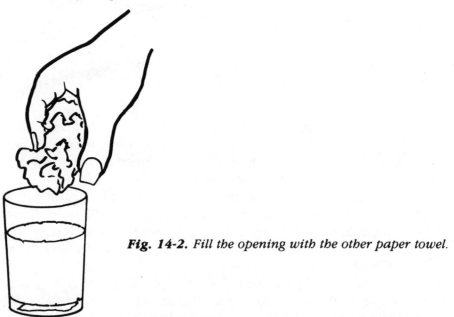

Fig. 14-2. *Fill the opening with the other paper towel.*

Fig. 14-3. *Place the bean between the paper towels and the glass.*

Fig. 14-4. *Completely wet the paper towels with water.*

Fig. 14-5. *The primary root begins to grow downward.*

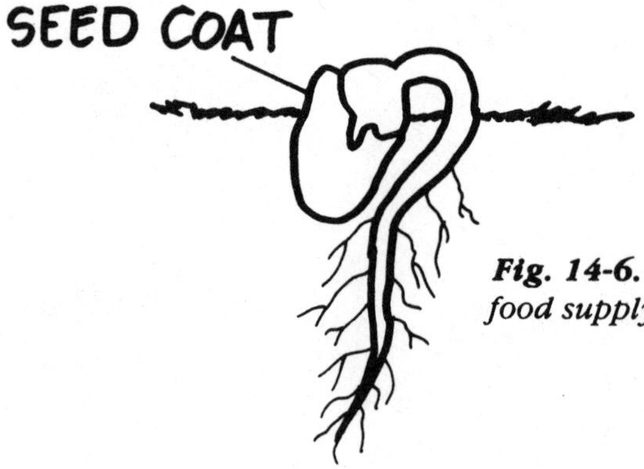

SEED COAT

Fig. 14-6. *The plant breaks through the surface, taking its food supply with it.*

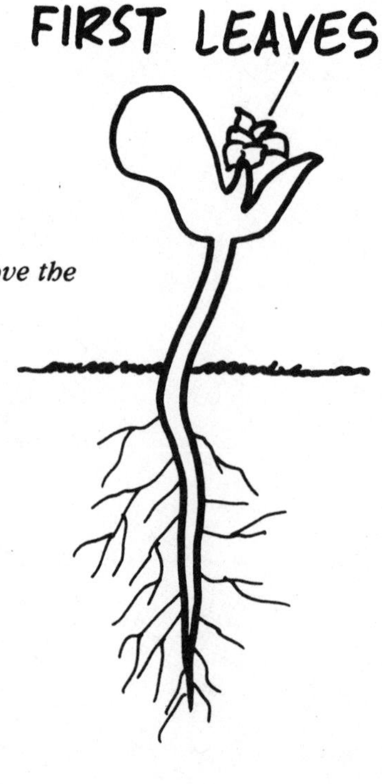

FIRST LEAVES

Fig. 14-7. *The cotyledons form the first leaves that appear above the ground.*

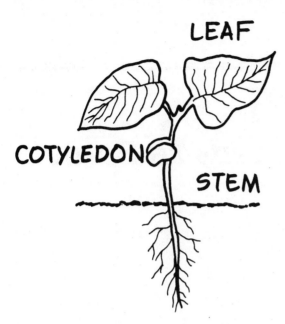

LEAF

COTYLEDON

STEM

Fig. 14-8. *The cotyledons store the food for the new plant.*

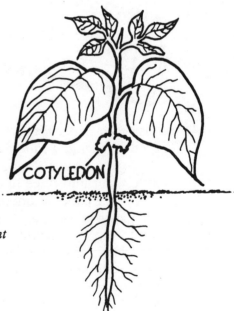

COTYLEDON

Fig. 14-9. *The real leaves of the new plant begin to develop.*

15
What a Seed Needs to Sprout

Materials

- 4 JARS
- 4 RUBBER BANDS
- PLASTIC FOOD WRAP
- 8 BEAN SEEDS
- 2 PAPER TOWELS
- WATER

Tear each paper towel in half so that you have four pieces. Fold each piece into a square that will fit in the bottom of the jars (Fig. 15-1). Place them flat against the bottom in each jar. Now pour a little water into three of the jars to completely wet the paper (Fig. 15-2). The paper in one jar should be kept dry. Place two beans on the paper in each jar (Fig. 15-3). Cover each jar with clear plastic food wrap and use rubber bands to hold it in place (Fig. 15-4).

Next, place the jar with dry paper and one with wet paper in a warm, sunny place. Put one jar with wet paper in the refrigerator, and the other jar with wet paper in a dark closet. You might want to number the jars and record the results. Number 1 could be labeled, "light and water." Number 2, "light and no water."

Number 3, "cold and water." Number 4, "no light with water" (Fig. 15-5). Notice the changes in the beans over the next several days.

Of the two jars in the sunny place, the seeds with water will be growing normally, and the ones without water will look just as they did when you put them in the jar. The seeds kept in the cold will be wrinkled but otherwise unchanged. The seeds kept in the dark, but with water, will have grown like the ones in the sun, except they will be completely white and have no color. These results tell you that plants need moisture, warmth and sunlight to develop.

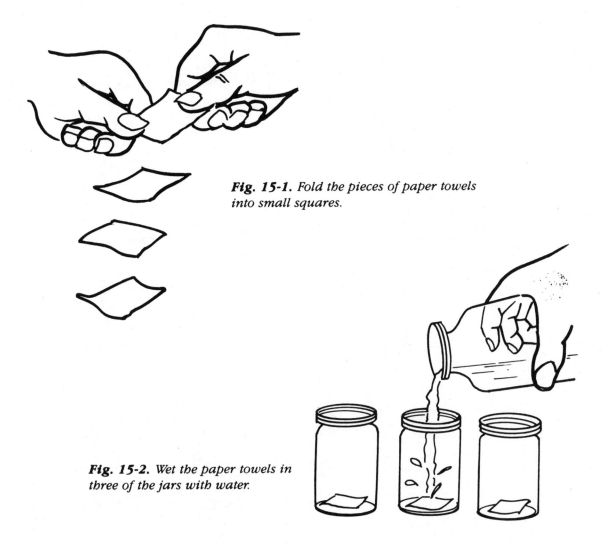

Fig. 15-1. Fold the pieces of paper towels into small squares.

Fig. 15-2. Wet the paper towels in three of the jars with water.

Fig. 15-3. *Place two beans in each of the jars.*

Fig. 15-4. *Cover each jar with plastic food wrap.*

Fig. 15-5. *Label each jar.*

1 LIGHT & WATER

2 LIGHT & NO WATER

3 COLD & WATER

4 NO LIGHT WITH WATER

16
How to Grow a Hanging Garden

Materials

- A FEW ROOT VEGETABLES (CARROTS, TURNIPS, RUTABAGAS, ETC.)
- TOOTHPICKS
- STRING
- CURTAIN ROD IN A SUNNY WINDOW
- KNIFE

Cut about 1/3 off of the top of the vegetable (Fig. 16-1) and turn the top so that the cut end is up. Carve or scoop out the center area to form a small bowl (Fig. 16-2). Next, insert three toothpicks, evenly spaced, in the side of the vegetable (Fig. 16-3). Attach strings to the toothpicks and hang the vegetable from the curtain rod in a sunny window (Fig. 16-4). Now fill the hollow part of the vegetable with water, and your vegetable will grow (Fig. 16-5). Keep the hole full of water and turn the plant now and then so that the leaves will grow evenly (Fig. 16-6).

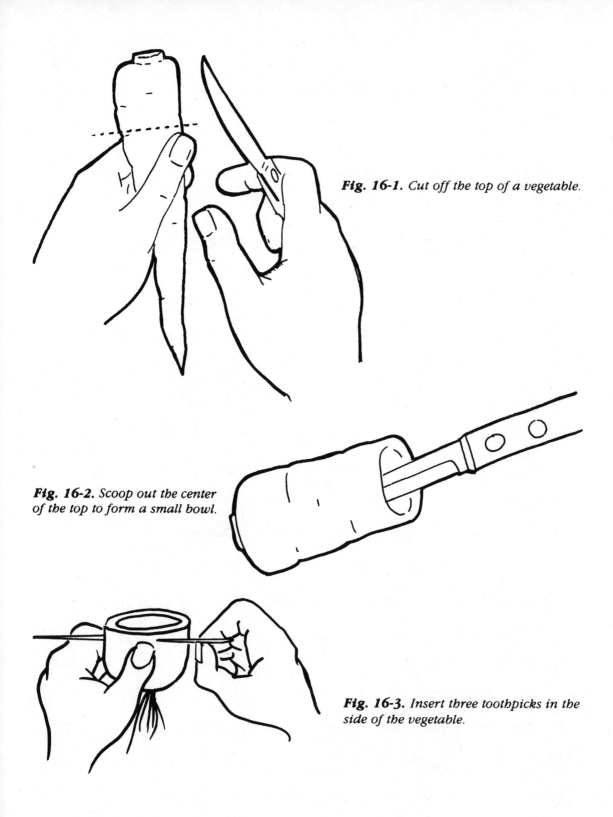

Fig. 16-1. *Cut off the top of a vegetable.*

Fig. 16-2. *Scoop out the center of the top to form a small bowl.*

Fig. 16-3. *Insert three toothpicks in the side of the vegetable.*

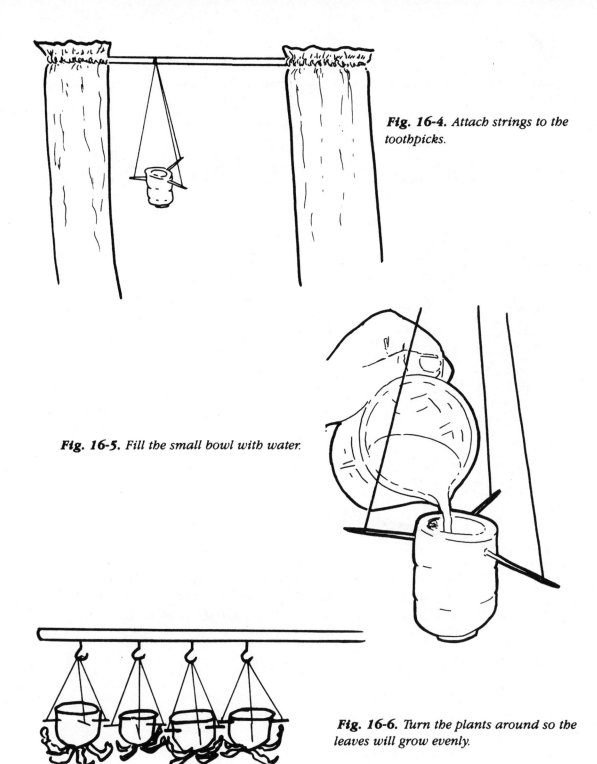

Fig. 16-4. *Attach strings to the toothpicks.*

Fig. 16-5. *Fill the small bowl with water.*

Fig. 16-6. *Turn the plants around so the leaves will grow evenly.*

17

How to Grow a Carrot Plant

Materials

- CARROT
- SAUCER
- DRINKING GLASS
- KNIFE
- WATER

Cut off about one inch from the top of the carrot (Fig. 17-1) and place the cut end of the carrot top down in a saucer of water (Fig. 17-2). Cover the piece of carrot with the glass (Fig. 17-3). When the leaves begin to grow, remove the glass (Fig. 17-4).

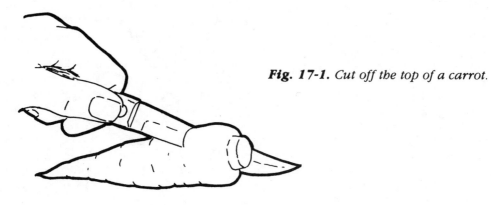

Fig. 17-1. *Cut off the top of a carrot.*

Fig. 17-2. *Place the top of the carrot in a saucer of water.*

Fig. 17-3. *Cover the carrot to keep in moisture.*

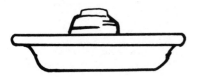

Fig. 17-4. Remove the glass when the leaves begin to grow.

PART VII

ENGINEERING

1

Gravity and Falling Bodies

Place the pillow on the floor. Hold the book in one hand and the paper in the other hand. Both objects should be level. Hold the book over the pillow (Fig. 1-1). Now drop them both at the same time. The book will hit the pillow first. Try the experiment again, but this time, place the paper flat on top of the book (Fig. 1-2). You will see that they both hit the pillow at the same time.

This result means that in the first try, the resistance of the air slowed the falling speed of the paper. But the second time, using gravity alone, you could see that light and heavy objects fall at the same speed.

Fig. 1-1. *Drop the book and the paper from the same height.*

Fig. 1-2. *Place the paper on top of the book.*

2
Paper Helicopter

Materials

- STRIP OF PAPER (ABOUT 2 INCHES WIDE AND 10 INCHES LONG)
- SCOTCH TAPE
- SCISSORS

Fold the paper in half lengthwise (Fig. 2-1). Make about 10 small bends in one end for weight. Fasten these bends in place with scotch tape (Fig. 2-2). At the other end of the strip, carefully cut down the center of the fold about 4 inches, and bend the two strips out to form narrow wings (Fig. 2-3).

Drop the helicopter from above your head, and it will rotate, slowing its descent. The weighted end creates the center of gravity. Air flowing past the wings cause them to rotate, slowing the rate of fall. Helicopters operate on this principle, and it is the reason that they are called rotary-wing aircraft.

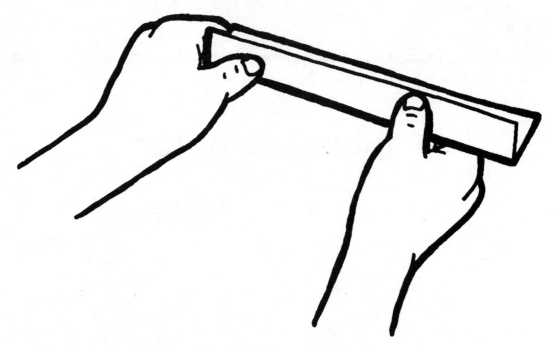

Fig. 2-1. _Fold the paper in half._

Fig. 2-2. _Fasten the bends in place with tape._

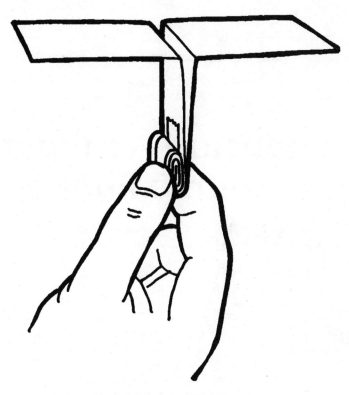

Fig. 2-3. *Fold the strips down for wings.*

3
Reducing Air Pressure with a Funnel

Materials

- SMALL FUNNEL
- MATCH
- CANDLE

With the help of an adult, carefully light the candle (Fig. 3-1) and hold the large opening of the funnel near the flame. Now try to blow out the flame by blowing through the small end of the funnel (Fig. 3-2). The flame will bend toward the open end of the funnel and will be very hard to blow out. If you turn the funnel around and blow through the wide end, you can blow out the candle easily (Fig. 3-3).

When you blew through the small end, the airstream traveled from the narrow part of the funnel to the larger area where it was forced to spread out. This spreading out of the air lowered the air pressure in the opening and caused the surrounding air, which was at a higher pressure, to move toward the open end of the funnel.

Fig. 3-1. *Use a candle to show the flow of air.*

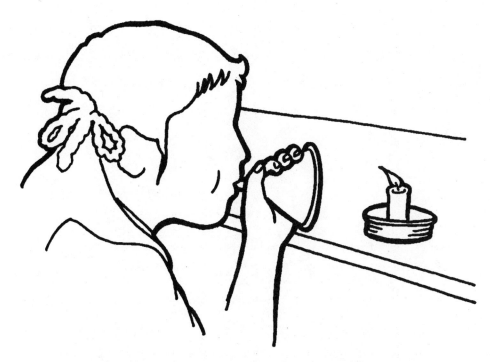

Fig. 3-2. *Blow through the small end of the funnel.*

Fig. 3-3. *Blow through the large end of the funnel.*

4

What Makes an Airfoil?

Materials

- SHEET OF PAPER (ABOUT 3 INCHES WIDE AND 10 INCHES LONG)
- SCOTCH TAPE
- PIECE OF CARDBOARD
- ELECTRIC FAN

Fold the paper in half so it is about 5 inches long. Hold the ends together, and then slide the top one down slightly so that the paper bends into a narrow loop (Fig. 4-1). Now tape the ends to the cardboard (Fig. 4-2). This makes the bottom of the loop flat with the cardboard and the top half curved. With the help of an adult, plug the fan in and turn it on. Hold the cardboard in the breeze from the fan. Have the taped ends pointing into the wind (Fig. 4-3). The paper airfoil will try to lift from the cardboard. The airfoil is able to lift because air flowing over the curved top is moving fast while the air below hardly is moving. This air flow reduces the air pressure in the area above the curved surface and creates the lifting force. This principle allows the wings to lift an airplane into the air.

Fig. 4-1. *Fold the paper into an airfoil.*

Fig. 4-2. *Tape the airfoil to a piece of cardboard.*

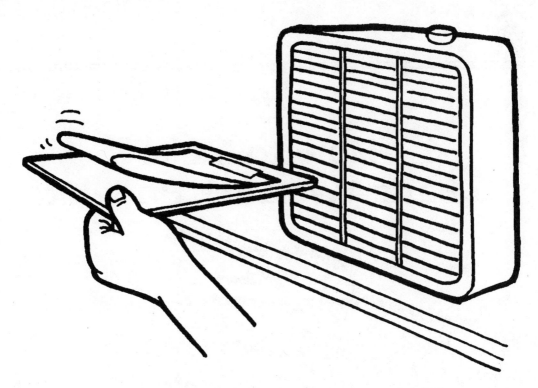

Fig. 4-3. *The breeze from the fan will cause the airfoil to lift.*

5

How to Make a Basic Two-Stick Bow Kite

Materials

- 2 PINE OR SPRUCE STICKS (1/4 X 3/8 INCH AND 36 INCHES LONG)
- COVERING MATERIAL (PLASTIC FROM LEAF, TRASH OR GARMENT BAG)
- STRING

Materials

- YARD STICK
- SMALL SAW
- SCISSORS
- SCOTCH TAPE OR MASKING TAPE
- PENCIL AND CHALK
- WOOD GLUE

With an adult's help, use the saw to notch the ends of both sticks (Fig. 5-1). Do not cut toward yourself. Measure and mark the center of one of the sticks, and place this point under the other stick 8 inches from one end (Fig. 5-2). Glue the sticks together, and bind the joint with a few wraps of string (Fig. 5-3). Stretch a framing string through the notches in the ends of the sticks to form the outer edge of the kite (Fig. 5-4). Pull the string tight, and tie the ends together with a square knot. Fasten the framing string in place by wrapping a couple of wraps of string around the notch on each side of the framing string (Fig. 5-5). The frame of the kite is now complete.

Place the frame on top of the plastic film to form a pattern. The cross stick should be on the side next to the plastic covering. Use the chalk to mark out the pattern (Fig. 5-6). Mark about an inch outside the framing string on all sides to allow for the flap to fold over the string. Carefully cut out the pattern and fold the flaps over the string. Fasten the flap in place with tape (Fig. 5-7). Now tie a piece of string to the notch in one end of the cross stick. Bow the cross stick until it has about a 4 inch bow, and tie the string in the notch in the other end of the stick (Fig. 5-8). To attach a bridle string, have an adult help you make a small hole where the two sticks cross. Use a piece of string about 5 feet long, and feed one end through the hole. Tie this end around both sticks. Tie the other end of the bridle string through the notch at the bottom of the kite. Tie the string used for flying to the bridle string at a point about 3 feet from the bottom of the kite and about 2 feet from where you connected the bridle string to the cross stick (Fig. 5-9). Shifting this point up or down just a little will adjust the flying angle of the kite. This kite should not require a tail and should fly easily in a light breeze. Always fly your kite in open areas away from power lines.

Fig. 5-1. *Notch the ends of the stick.*

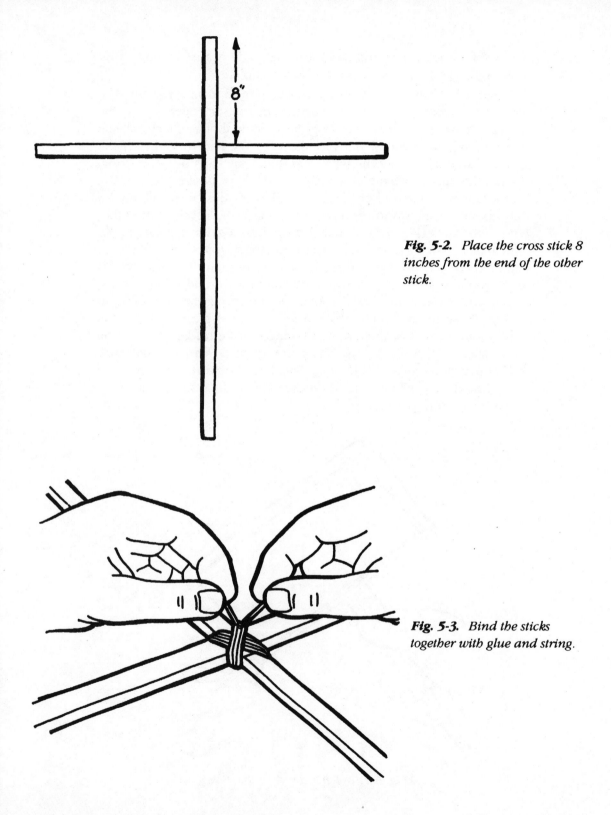

Fig. 5-2. *Place the cross stick 8 inches from the end of the other stick.*

Fig. 5-3. *Bind the sticks together with glue and string.*

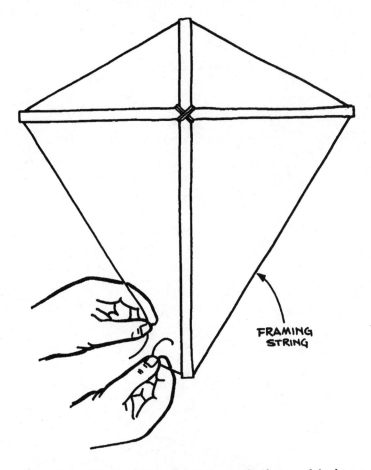

Fig. 5-4. *Attach the framing string to the frame of the kite.*

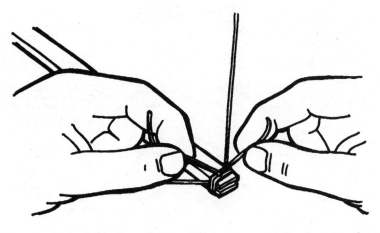

Fig. 5-5. *Hold the framing string in place with a couple of wraps of string.*

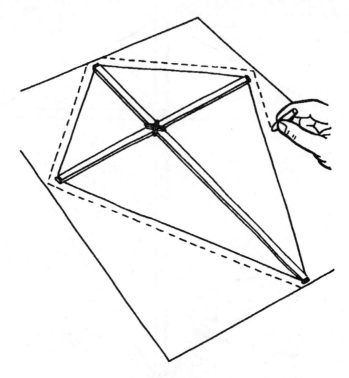

Fig. 5-6. *Mark out the pattern with chalk.*

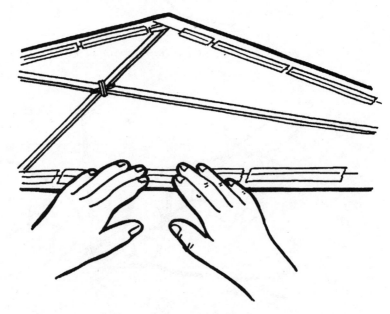

Fig. 5-7. *Fasten the flap in place with tape.*

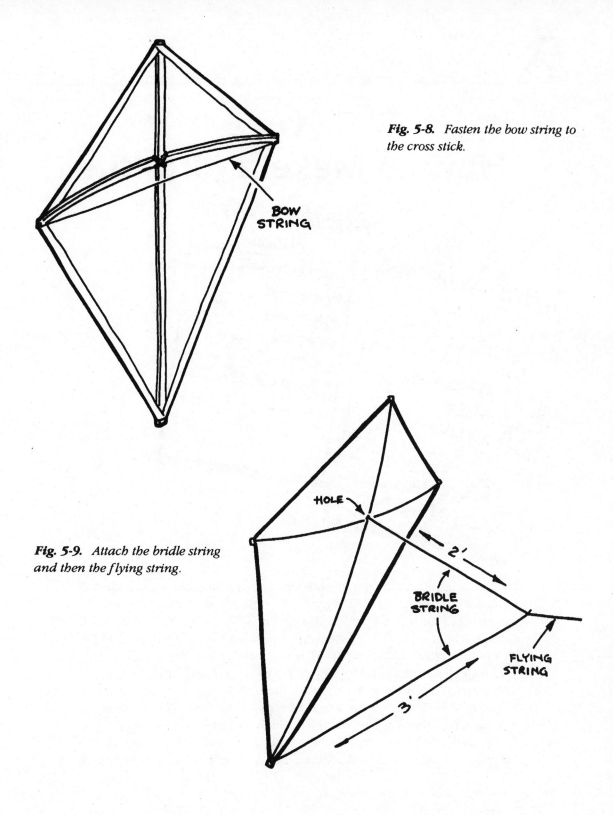

Fig. 5-8. Fasten the bow string to the cross stick.

Fig. 5-9. Attach the bridle string and then the flying string.

BOW STRING

HOLE

2'

BRIDLE STRING

FLYING STRING

3'

6
How to Make a Bird Kite

Materials

- 1 FLEXIBLE STICK 40 INCHES LONG
- 2 STICKS 26 INCHES LONG
- 1 STICK 10 INCHES LONG
- COVERING MATERIAL (PLASTIC OR PAPER)

Materials

- CELLOPHANE TAPE OR MASKING TAPE
- STRING
- SMALL SAW
- WOOD GLUE

With an adult's help, notch both ends of the flexible stick with the saw for the framing string (Fig. 6-1). Form a V with the two 26-inch sticks, and tie the pointed end together with string. Add a drop of glue to the joint to hold it securely. The other end of the V should be 14 inches apart. Place the 10-inch stick across the V about 9 inches from the open end. Fasten it in place with wraps of string (Fig. 6-2). Now place the 40-inch stick across the V, 5 inches from the pointed end. *Lash* it to the V with wraps of string (Fig. 6-3). Tie the framing string across the V just below the 10-inch stick, leaving enough string to reach the ends of the 40-inch stick. Bow the 40-inch stick back toward the open end of the V to a point 15 inches from the ends of the 10-inch stick. Tie the string here and run it over to the other side. Bow this tip back to match the first wing (15 inches) and tie the framing string through the notch in the bowed 40-inch stick. Next, stretch string across the open end of the V to form an X below the 10-inch stick (Fig. 6-4). Apply the covering material and fasten in place as in the previous experiment (Fig. 6-5). Attach the bridle by using five strings tied from each outer tip of the kite (Fig. 6-6). Tie the strings together about 14 inches from the front of the kite and about one-third of the way from the top. Some adjustment of the bridle might be necessary. You must have a tail of about 20 feet. You can attach the tail to a string running from the two tips at the bottom of the kite.

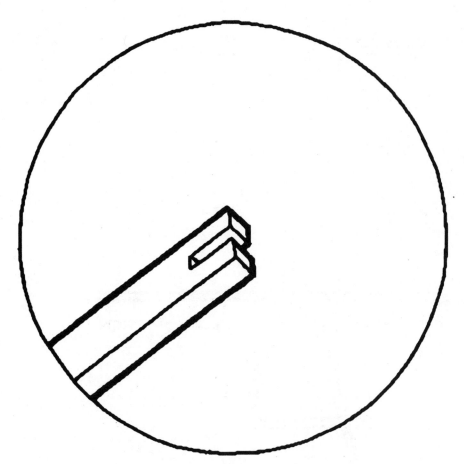

Fig. 6-1. *Notch both ends of the 40-inch stick.*

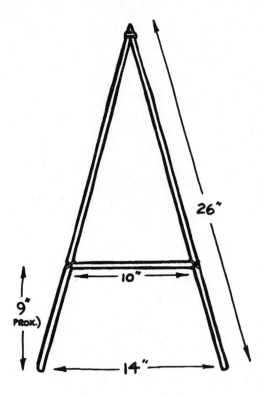

Fig. 6-2. *Build a frame as shown from the three remaining sticks.*

26"

10"

9" (PROX.)

14"

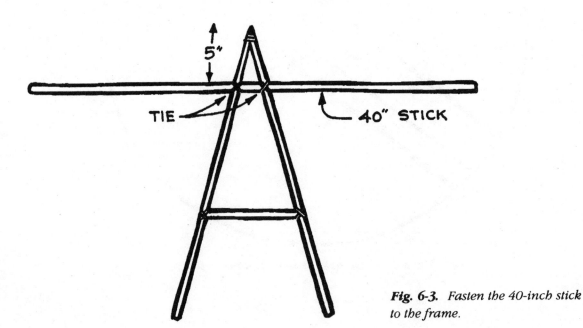

5"

TIE

40" STICK

Fig. 6-3. *Fasten the 40-inch stick to the frame.*

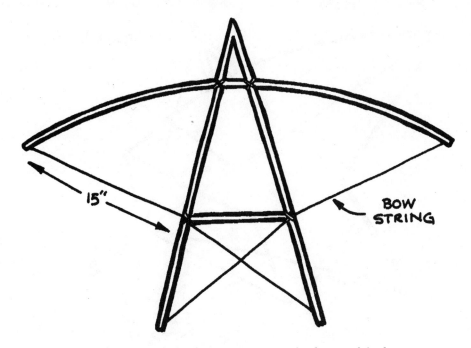

Fig. 6-4. *Attach the framing string to the frame of the kite.*

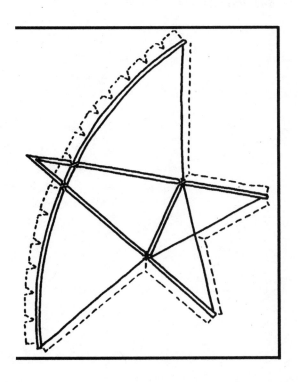

Fig. 6-5. *Mark the pattern on the covering material.*

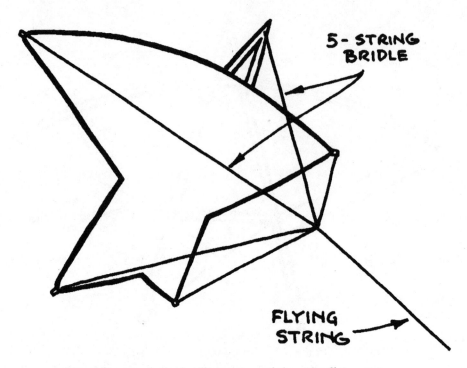

Fig. 6-6. *Attach the bridle string and then the flying string.*

7

How to Make a Wind Tunnel

With the help of an adult, carefully cut off both ends of each carton (Fig. 7-1) and stack them together in rows of three to form a large open box with dividers. Tape or glue the cartons together. Place an electric fan at one end of the wind tunnel and, with adult help, turn it on (Fig. 7-2). A smooth flow of air will come out the other end. A fan alone produces a twisting flow of air, but the partitions in your wind tunnel help stabilize the flow of air.

To test, hold a lightweight model airplane or piece of cardboard on a string at the end of the tunnel.

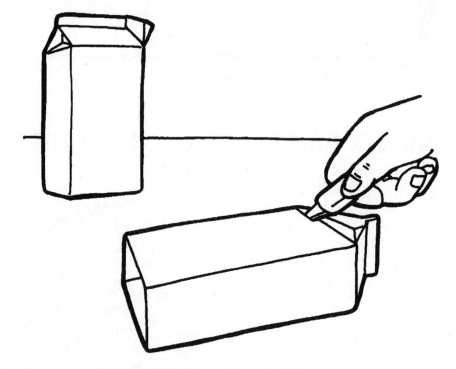

Fig. 7-1. *Carefully cut the ends off the cartons.*

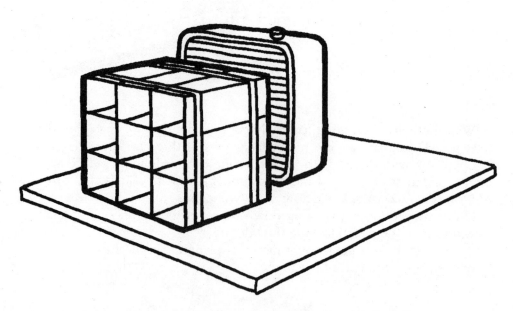

Fig. 7-2. *Fasten the cartons together with tape or glue.*

8

A Paper Airplane for Distance

Fold the paper as shown in Figs. 8-1, 8-2, and 8-3, and you will have an airplane designed for distance flight.

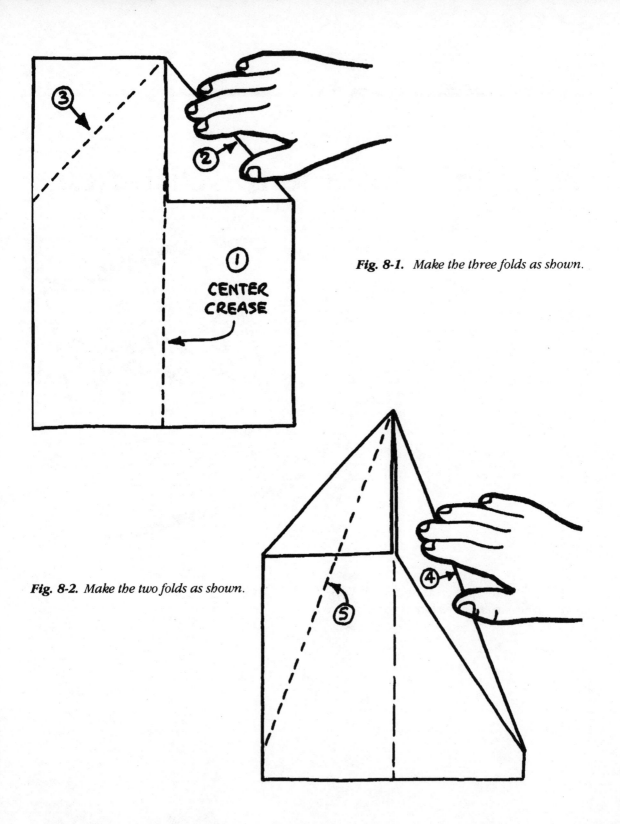

Fig. 8-1. Make the three folds as shown.

Fig. 8-2. Make the two folds as shown.

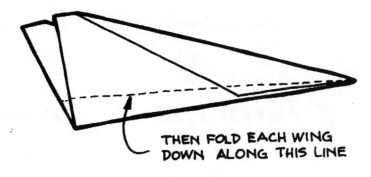

FOLD ON CENTER-LINE:

THEN FOLD EACH WING
DOWN ALONG THIS LINE

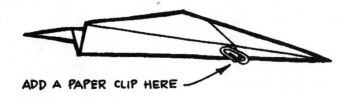

ADD A PAPER CLIP HERE

Fig. 8-3. *Fold down the wings and attach a paper clip for balance.*

9

A Paper Airplane for Duration

Materials
- SHEET OF PAPER (8 X 10 ¼ INCHES)
- SCISSORS

Complete the folds as shown in Figs. 9-1, 9-2, and 9-3 for an airplane designed for duration flying.

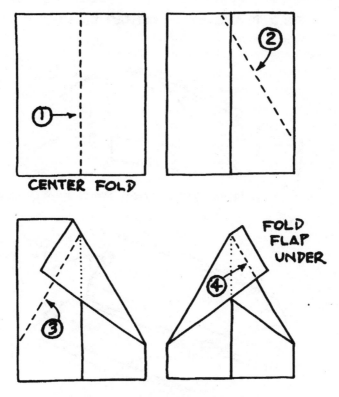

CENTER FOLD

FOLD
FLAP
UNDER

Fig. 9-1. *Make the four folds as shown.*

TURN PLANE OVER AND
FOLD BACK THE NOSE...

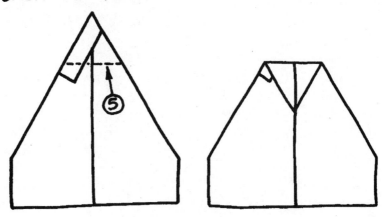

Fig. 9-2. *Make the fold for the nose.*

FOLD PLANE UP ON CENTER LINE:

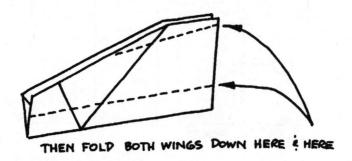

THEN FOLD BOTH WINGS DOWN HERE & HERE

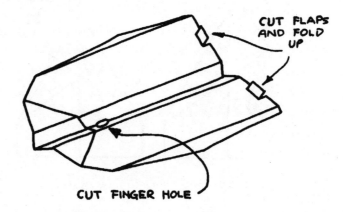

CUT FLAPS
AND FOLD
UP

CUT FINGER HOLE

Fig. 9-3. *Fold down the wings and make the cuts for the flaps.*

10

A Two-Ring Paper Airplane

Carefully cut two strips of paper about ½ inch wide and 11 inches long (Fig. 10-1). Make each strip into a ring, and use tape to hold the ends together (Fig. 10-2). Tape one of the rings to the side of the straw about two inches from one end. This side will be the front. Tape the other ring to the same side of the straw about one inch from the other end (Fig. 10-3). Launch the airplane into the air (Fig. 10-4). You can change the flight path by moving the rings to different positions on the straw.

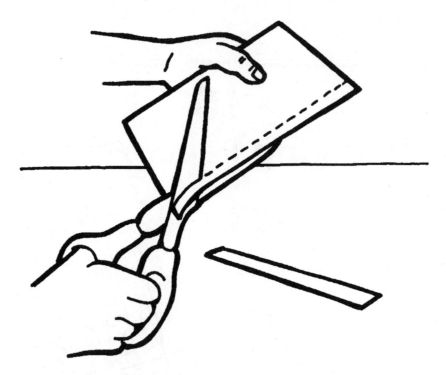

Fig. 10-1. *Cut off two strips of paper.*

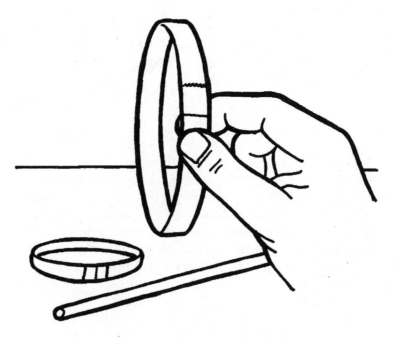

Fig. 10-2. *Form the strips into rings.*

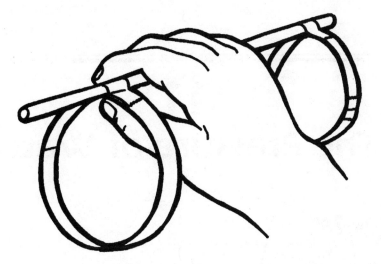

Fig. 10-3. *Fasten the rings to the straw.*

Fig. 10-4. *You can change the flight path by repositioning the rings.*

11

The Pressure of Water

Materials

- MILK CARTON
- CELLOPHANE
- TAPE
- NAIL
- WATER
- KITCHEN SINK

Have an adult help you punch three holes in the side of an empty milk carton with the nail. Punch one near the bottom, one about the middle, and one near the top (Fig. 11-1). Cover the holes with one long strip of tape (Fig. 11-2). Now fill the carton with water all the way to the top (Fig. 11-3). Place the carton near the edge of the sink with the holes pointing toward the drain, and remove the tape (Fig. 11-4). The stream of water from the top hole will not spurt out very far. The water from the lower hole will spurt a little farther, and the water from the bottom hole will travel the farthest. Water pressure depends on the depth of the water. The stream from each hole has the pressure of the amount of water above that hole. This concept is why some cities have their water supply in raised tanks. It provides water pressure for the water system.

Fig. 11-1. *Make three holes in the carton.*

Fig. 11-2. *Cover the holes with tape.*

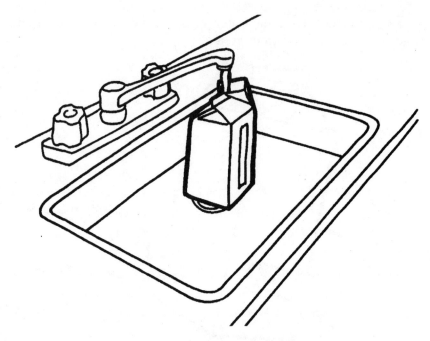

Fig. 11-3. *Fill the carton with water.*

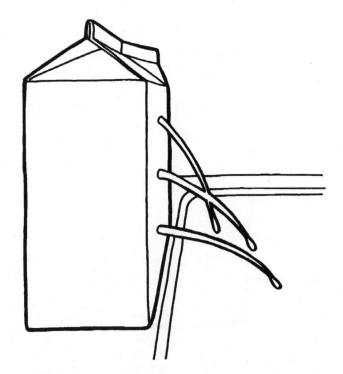

Fig. 11-4. *The deeper the water, the more pressure it has.*

12
Water Pressure and the Size of the Container

With an adult watching, use the nail to punch a hole in the side of each container, one inch from the bottom, and cover each hole with tape (Fig. 12-1). Fill the smaller can with water and fill the larger container to the same level as the smaller can (Fig. 12-2). Place both containers at the edge of the sink with the holes facing the drain and remove the tapes. The streams of water will spurt out the same distance from their containers (Fig. 12-3). You can see that water pressure depends only on the depth of the water and not on the size or shape of the container.

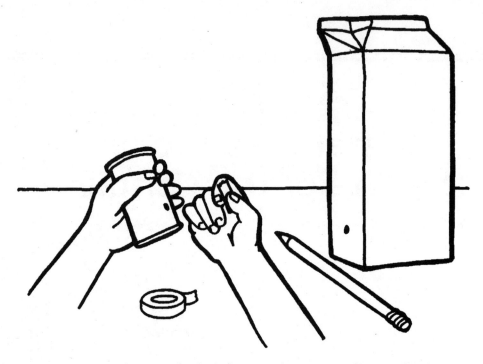

Fig. 12-1. *Make the holes in each container the same height.*

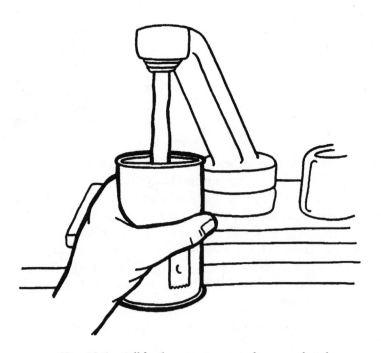

Fig. 12-2. *Fill both containers to the same height.*

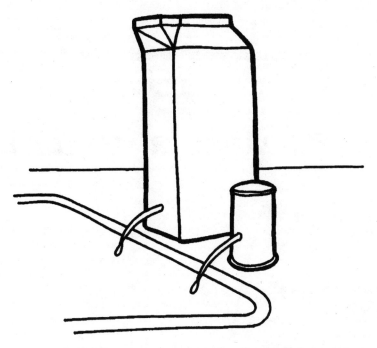

Fig. 12-3. *The water pressure is the same in both containers.*

13

How to Make a Water Level

Use the string to attach one end of the hose to a point on the fence (Fig. 13-1). The open end of the hose should be pointing straight up. Now lay the hose along the fence and bring the other end up to a point about the same height (Fig. 13-2). Use string to hold it in place. Use the funnel to completely fill the hose with water (Fig. 13-3).

Raise or lower one end of the hose until the water is flush with both openings. When this is done, a string stretched between the two ends will be level (Fig. 13-4). Pressure pushes on both ends of the hose equally, so the level of the water in each end will be the same.

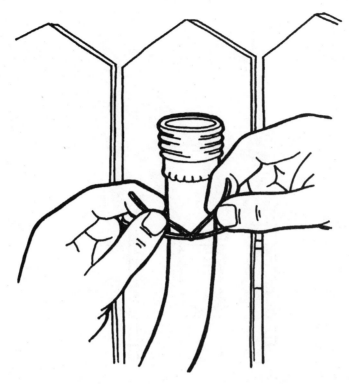

Fig. 13-1. *Fasten the hose to a point above the ground.*

Fig. 13-2. *Fasten the other end of the hose to a point about the same height.*

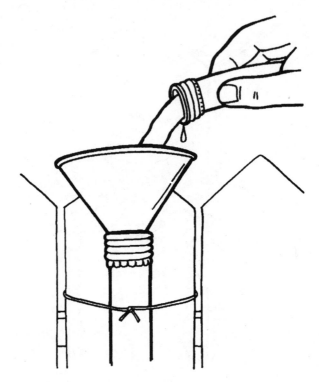

Fig. 13-3. *Fill the hose with water.*

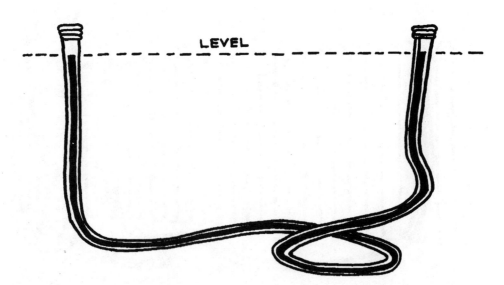

Fig. 13-4. *The water level in each end of the hose will be at the same height.*

14

How to Measure Water Pressure

Materials
- CLEAR PLASTIC TUBING (ABOUT 5 FEET LONG)
- FUNNEL
- BUSTED BALLOON
- STRING
- CELLOPHANE TAPE
- WIRE (FROM COAT HANGER)

Materials
- FOOD COLORING
- WATER
- BUCKET
- FELT PEN

Have an adult cut a coat hanger for you. Be careful of sharp ends. Bend the wire into a stand to support an 18-inch length of tubing shaped into a U (Fig. 14-1). Fasten the tubing in place with tape. Fill this U-shaped tubing halfway up with colored water.

Now press the end of the funnel into the other end of the tubing. Cover the wide opening in the funnel with a layer of rubber from the balloon. Stretch the rubber *taut* and fasten it tightly in place with string (Fig. 14-2).

Now watch the level of the colored water as you place the funnel upside down in the bucket of water (Fig. 14-3). Notice the level when the funnel is just below the surface of the water, when it's halfway down, and then when it's near the bottom of the bucket. You will see that the colored water moves closer to the open end of the tubing as the funnel goes deeper into the water. This happens because water pressure increases as the water becomes deeper.

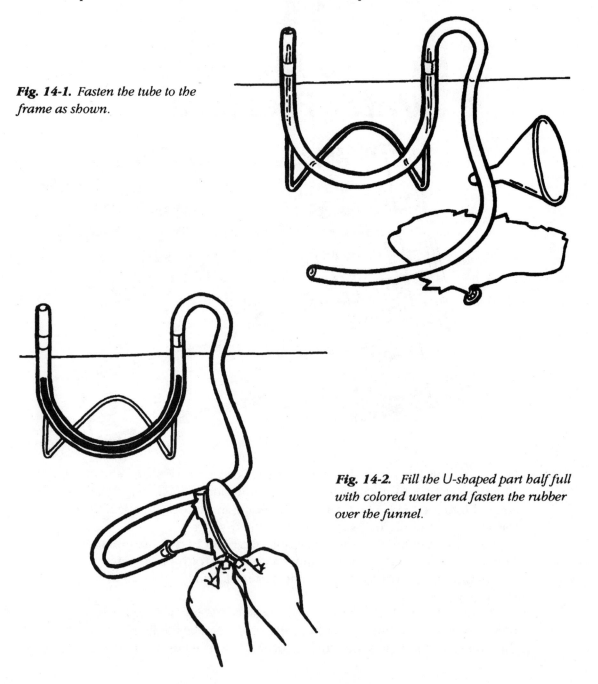

Fig. 14-1. *Fasten the tube to the frame as shown.*

Fig. 14-2. *Fill the U-shaped part half full with colored water and fasten the rubber over the funnel.*

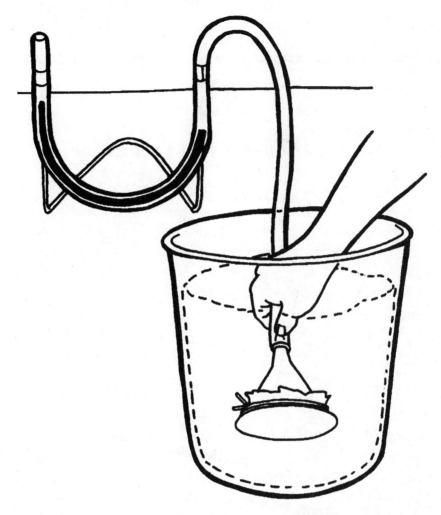

Fig. 14-3. *Water pressure in the bucket causes the colored water to move.*

15
Fountain in a Jar

Materials

- 2 JARS (ONE WITH SCREW-TYPE LID)
- 2 PLASTIC DRINKING STRAWS
- MODELING CLAY
- WATER
- LARGE NAIL AND HAMMER

Materials

- RULER
- SCISSORS
- KITCHEN SINK

With the help of an adult, use the nail and hammer to punch two holes in the lid of the jar the size of the straws. Push the end of one of the straws about ½ inch through one of the holes and the other straw about 2 inches through the other hole (Fig. 15-1). Cut the second straw so that about 4 inches sticks above the lid. Use the clay to seal the openings around the straws. Now fill the jar about half full of water and screw the lid in place (Fig. 15-2). Fill the other jar with water and place it near the edge of the sink. Quickly turn the jar with the lid upside down and lower the shorter straw into the water in the other jar. You will see a fountain of water appear in the upper jar (Fig. 15-3). The fountain occurred because the water flowing from the longer straw reduced the air pressure inside the closed jar. The higher air pressure on the water in the open jar pushed the water up the short straw and created the fountain.

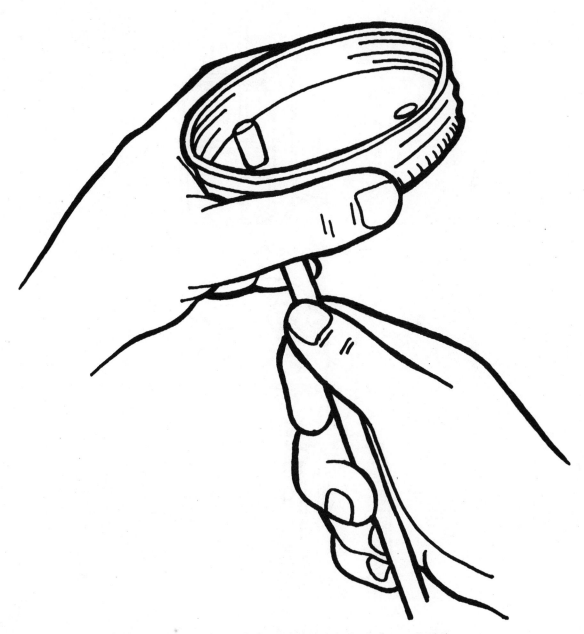

Fig. 15-1. *Push the straws through the holes in the lid.*

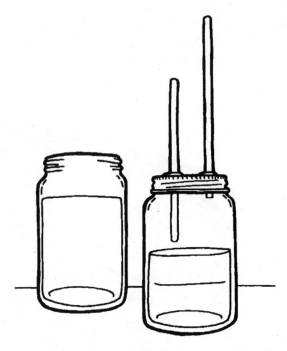

Fig. 15-2. *Fill the jar about half full of water and replace the lid.*

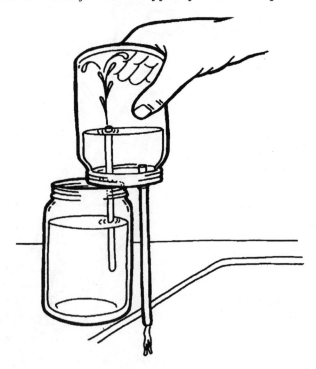

Fig. 15-3. *Water flowing from the straw causes a fountain to appear in the jar.*

16
Water and Friction

Materials

- 2 JARS THE SAME SIZE WITH LIDS
- A SHALLOW RAMP (BOARD WITH ONE END RAISED)
- WATER

Fill one of the jars about half full with water, and screw the lid on tight (Fig. 16-1). Place both jars at the top of the ramp and release them at the same time (Fig. 16-2). You will see that the jar with the water will start faster but the empty jar will roll farther when they reach the level area past the ramp. The jar with the water slowed down because of the friction between the water and the sides of the jar. The air in the empty jar produced no friction.

Fig. 16-1. *Fill one jar about half full of water.*

Fig. 16-2. *Water in the one jar will create friction.*

17
Why a Sprinkler Turns

With adult help, use the hammer and nail to punch four holes an equal distance around the can near the bottom (Fig. 17-1). As you remove the nail from each hole, push the nail to one side to aim the hole at an angle (Fig. 17-2). Aim all holes in the same direction. Now bend the tab at the top of the can straight up and tie one end of the string in the tab opening (Fig. 17-3). Place the can in the sink and fill it with water. Now lift the can by the string, and it will quickly begin to spin as water spurts from the holes (Fig. 17-4).

For every action, there is an equal and opposite reaction. In this case, the water spurts from the can at an angle, and because the can is suspended by a string, offering very little resistance, the force of the flowing water causes the can to rotate. Water shooting from a nozzle creates a similar force. If the nozzle is free to turn, as in a sprinkler, it will rotate.

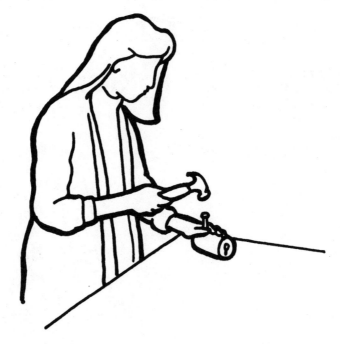

Fig. 17-1. *Punch holes near the bottom of the can.*

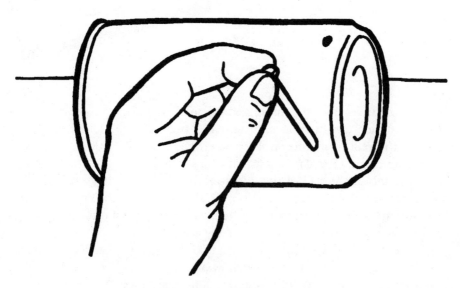

Fig. 17-2. *Bend the holes at an angle.*

Fig. 17-3. *Attach a string to the tab.*

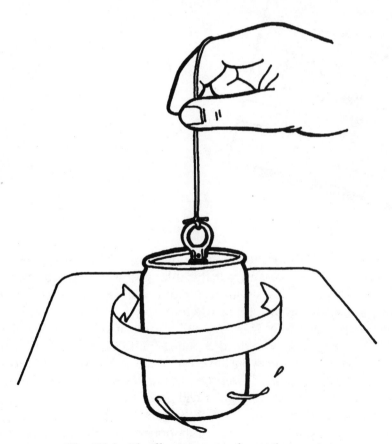

Fig. 17-4. *The flowing water forces the can to turn.*

18

Adding Weight to Water

Tie one end of the string through the nut (Fig. 18-1). Next, place the pencil on a flat surface and put the ruler halfway across the pencil (Fig. 18-2). Fill the glasses with water and balance them on the ruler. Balancing the glasses will be nearly impossible, but get as close to a balance as possible (Fig. 18-3). It will be easier if you place the glasses on the ruler, and, holding the pencil with one finger, adjust the pencil to balance. When you have one glass just about ready to go down, hold the string and lower the nut into the water without touching the glass (Fig. 18-4). The glass will go down.

The balance is upset because of the extra weight. The nut weighs less in water, and the difference in its normal weight and the lower weight is added to the water.

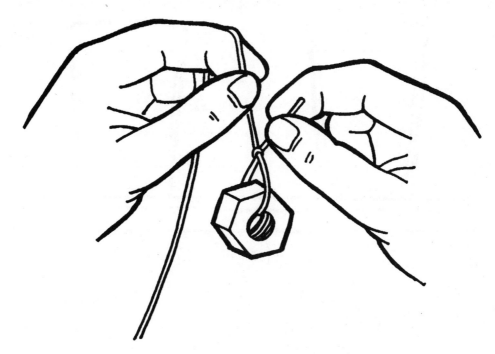

Fig. 18-1. *Tie a string to the weight.*

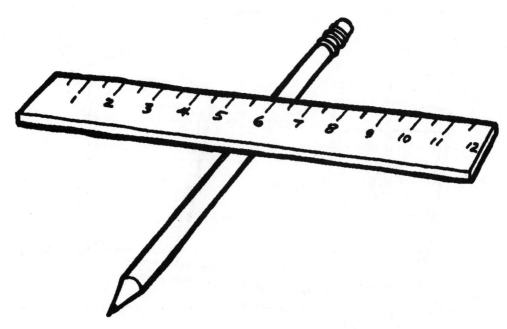

Fig. 18-2. *Place the ruler across the pencil.*

Fig. 18-3. *Try to balance the glasses.*

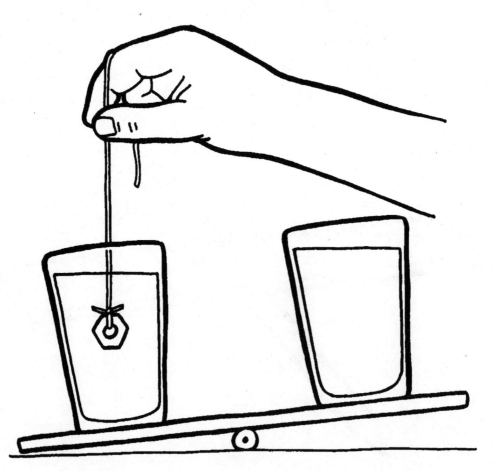

Fig. 18-4. *The extra weight causes the balance to tilt.*

19

How a Ramp Overcomes Force

Prop the ends of the yardstick and the ruler on the books to make two ramps. One ramp should be steeper than the other (Fig. 19-1). Loop three rubber bands together (Fig. 19-2) and use the tack to attach one end to the block (Fig. 19-3). Be careful not to poke yourself with the tack. Now lift the block straight up by the rubber bands and notice how far they stretch (Fig. 19-4). Next, drag the block up the steeper ramp and see how far the rubber bands stretch. Then try the longer ramp (Fig. 19-5). You can see that the rubber bands stretched the most when you lifted the block straight up. Then they stretched less and less as the ramps became longer and flatter. The ramp is called an *inclined plane* and can be thought of as a machine that reduces work. You use less force, but the block must travel farther.

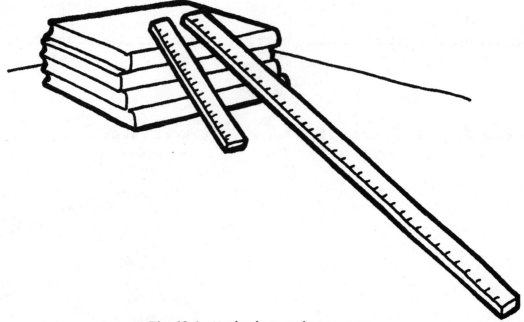

Fig. 19-1. *Use books to make two ramps.*

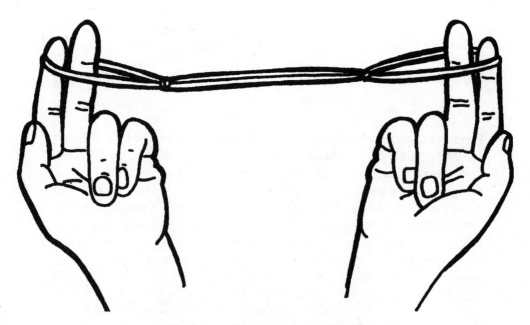

Fig. 19-2. *Loop rubber bands together.*

Fig. 19-3. *Fasten the rubber bands to the block of wood.*

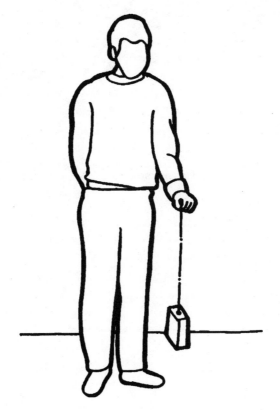

Fig. 19-4. *Notice how far the rubber bands stretch.*

Fig. 19-5. *It takes less force to move the block up the longer ramp.*

20
The Screw and the Ramp

Examine the screw and notice how the threads are angled (Fig. 20-1). Now cut a triangle, or ramp, from the sheet of paper. Use the marker to mark along the cut edge, or the ramp (Fig. 20-2). Roll the paper onto the pencil from one short side of the triangle to the opposite point (Fig. 20-3). Keep the bottom, or baseline, of the triangle even as it rolls.

The colored edge, marking the ramp, will spiral up the pencil forming the pattern of a screw (Fig. 20-4). You can see that a screw is actually an inclined plane.

Fig. 20-1. *Notice that the threads on the screw are angled.*

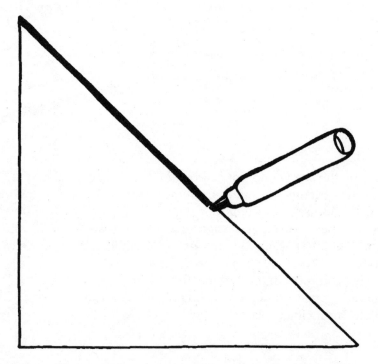

Fig. 20-2. *Mark the ramp part of the triangle.*

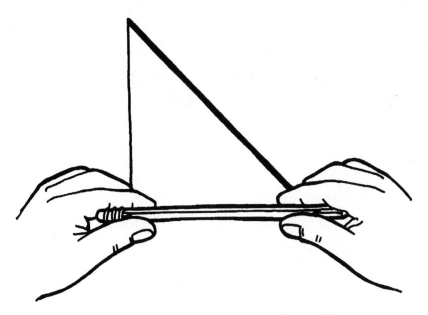

Fig. 20-3. Roll the paper onto the pencil.

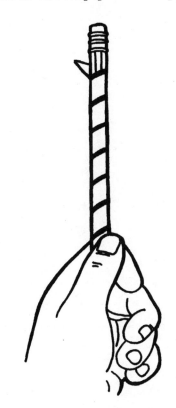

Fig. 20-4. Angle the marked edge like the threads on the screw.

Science Fair Projects

A science fair project can be an exciting learning experience, but it does require some planning. Not enough to fret over but a little organization and planning is necessary if you want the project to be successful. One of the most important parts of the planning stage is deciding on the subject. Do some research and give the subject a lot of thought. If you choose a subject too quickly, you might discover later that the materials are too expensive or not even available, or that the project was just too complicated to complete. When this happens, it is too easy to abandon the project and it is usually too late to start another.

You may want to start by dividing your science fair project into four easy steps:

1. Choosing a subject.

2. Questions and hypothesis. A hypothesis is just what you think the results of the experiment will be—a well-thought-out guess.

3. Doing the experiment.

4. The results and your conclusions.

You might want to write a research paper (Fig. 1). The research paper will help you gather important information and narrow down your subject to a specific topic. You probably want to make a report on your experiment. This is to show what you wanted to prove or

Fig. 1. A research paper will help you gather information.

a question you wanted answered. You can use graphs and charts to help explain your project. The report should describe your experiment, the results of your experiment, and the conclusions you formed based on the results of the experiment.

When deciding on a project, pick a subject that you are really interested in, or one that you would like to learn more about. Choose a subject that you are enthused about, but not one that is too complicated. You might find problems locating the materials. A simple, well demonstrated experiment can be much more successful than a complicated one not performed well. Often, major scientific breakthroughs are discovered using simple equipment.

Materials for experiments can often be throwaway items found around the home, such as empty coffee cans, plastic or glass bottles, cardboard tubes from paper towels, or empty wooden spools from sewing thread (Fig. 2).

Fig. 2. *Throwaway items can often be used in experiments.*

You might want to build a model. Usually, these can be made from wood or cardboard. You have to be creative and use your imagination.

Once you have selected the subject of your project, choose a specific question to be answered or a point to prove. Don't generalize. Have a definite problem to solve.

You probably will want to display your experiment on a table. It could be set up in front of cardboard or wooden panels (Fig. 3).

The panels could be in three sections. The two end sections might be angled forward so that the panel stands by itself, like the back part of a theater stage. The panel sections can show the information from your report. The left section could show the purpose of your experiment. This could include why you chose the project or what you wanted to prove. The middle section of the panel could show how your experiment was constructed and why it was built the way it was. The right section of the panel could show the results of your experiment and the conclusions you've made. It could also include any possible uses, or applications for, this information.

Fig. 3. *Posters mounted on the panel will help explain your experiment.*

If you use your imagination, you can expand and develop any simple experiment into a very interesting and educational project. Most any experiment will probably have been done before, but yours might be just a little different. Try to use a different point of view, or change a known experiment so that you prove something completely different. The important part of a science fair project is to have fun while you discover something new.

Glossary

acid   A compound that can react with a base to form a salt.

air mass   A huge mass of cold or warm air that moves around the world. It can be moist or dry.

airfoil   A device with a curved surface, such as an airplane wing, designed to create lift.

acceleration   The rate of change of velocity in a moving body.

alabaster   White, translucent gypsum with fine texture.

algae   Simple plants with no true stem, root, or leaf.

alkalis   Any soluble mineral salt, or mixture of salts, found in soil and capable of neutralizing **acids**.

alloys   A mixture of two or more metals.

altitude   The angular distance above the horizon; the distance up from the ground.

altocumulus cloud   A formation of white or gray clouds in many shapes, most commonly rounded, found at intermediate heights.

altostratus cloud   A formation of gray to bluish clouds at intermediate heights in continuous dense layers or thick patches.

anticlines   Shapely arched folds of stratified rock, from whose central axis the strata slope downward in opposite directions; opposed to synclines.

arteries   Tubelike blood vessels that carry blood from the heart to other parts of the body.

astrolabe   An instrument formerly used to find the altitude of a star, etc.; it was replaced by the sextant.

atmosphere The mass of air, clouds, gases, and vapor, surrounding the earth.

atmospheric pressure The pressure caused by gravity of the blanket of air around the earth.

atom Any of the smallest particles of an element that combine with similar particles of other elements to produce **compounds**.

average The result obtained by dividing a sum by the number of quantities added; in extended use it is applied to the usual or ordinary kind.

barometer An instrument for measuring atmospheric pressure. It is helpful in determining weather changes.

base A substance which forms a salt when it reacts with an **acid**.

bauxite The claylike ore, i.e., hydrated aluminum oxide, from which aluminum is obtained.

biosphere The zone of the earth, extending from its crust out into the surrounding atmosphere that supports life.

blood veins Vessels conveying blood back to the heart from the various organs of the body.

calcination The process of heating to a high temperature.

calcium A soft, silver-white, metallic chemical element found in limestone, marble, and chalk.

calibrate To fix, check, or correct the graduations of a measuring instrument, such as a thermometer.

capillaries Tiny tubes that carry blood from the arteries to the veins.

capillary action The movement caused by surface tension and other forces of a liquid through tiny openings in a solid.

carbohydrates Certain organic compounds, including sugar, starch, and celluloses. They make up an important class of food in animal nutrition by supplying energy to the body.

carbon dioxide A colorless, odorless, nonflammable gas, somewhat heavier than air, that passes out of the lungs in breathing.

Celsius Degrees (C) used for measuring temperature, also called centigrade.

center of gravity That point in a body or system around which weight is distributed evenly or balanced.

centigrade See **Celsius**.

centrifugal force The force tending to pull a thing outward when it is rotating rapidly around a center.

centripetal force The force tending to pull a thing inward when it is rotating rapidly around a center.

chloride The compound in which chlorine is combined with another element.

chlorophyll The matter in plants causing the green coloring.

circumference The line marking the boundary of a circle or a rounded surface.

cirrus cloud A formation of clouds in detached, wispy filaments, or feathery tufts, at heights above 20,000 feet. They are often signs of bad weather to come.

cloud A visible mass of condensed water vapor suspended in the **atmosphere** and consisting of minute droplets of water or ice crystals.

cold fronts Boundaries between two different air masses caused when cold air pushes warm air away; usually means colder weather is approaching.

compound A material made up of two or more elements joined together.

concentrated Collected or focused where the strength, or density, is increased.

condensation The act of condensing, such as a reduction of a gas to a liquid.

condense To change a substance to a denser form, such as from a gas to a liquid.

continental drift The theory that continents slowly shift their positions as a result of currents in the molten rocks beneath the earth's crust.

continents The biggest land masses on earth. The continents are Africa, Antarctica, Asia, Australia, Europe, North America, and South America.

contour line An imaginary line connecting points on the ground with the same elevation above a reference plane.

contract Shrink in size.

convection currents Currents that flow when lighter, warm air rises and heavier, cool air flows in to take its place.

Coriolis force The force created by the bending of the winds caused by the earth spinning on its axis.

corrosion The gradual wearing away, as by rusting or by action of chemicals.

cotyledons The first leaves that sprout from a seed. They manufacture food for the new plant.

cumulonimbus cloud A dense cloud towering to great heights, with the upper portion usually flattened. Often produces lightning and heavy showers.

cumulus cloud A thick cloud, usually isolated, with a dark, nearly horizontal base. The upper parts resemble domes or towers.

delta A deposit of sand and soil, usually triangular, formed at the mouth of some rivers.

depression contour line An imaginary line connecting points on the ground with the same elevation below a reference plane.

dew point The temperature at which **condensation** begins to form because the air cannot hold any more water vapor.

diaphragm The partition of muscles and tendons between the chest cavity and the abdominal cavity; the midriff.

distilled Something that has been refined or made more nearly pure by first heating and then allowing to cool and condense.

downdraft A downward flow of air caused by **convection currents** or the down-wind side of mountains.

Earth's magnetic field The magnetic force surrounding the earth from the magnetic north pole to the magnetic south pole.

elasticity   Quality of being elastic.

electromagnetism   A force that travels in waves through space that include radio, visible light, and X-ray waves; the branch of physics that studies electricity and magnetism.

element   A material made up of only one kind of atom.

energy   Force of expression or utterance; strength or power efficiently exerted.

enzyme   A protein-like substance found in plants and animals that speeds up specific chemical reactions.

equator   An imaginary circle around the earth, equally distant at all points from both the north pole and the south pole; zero degree latitude.

equatorial low   A low pressure area caused by the warm air rising over the equator.

erosion   The wearing away of land or rock by wind or water.

evaporate   To change a liquid into a vapor.

evaporation   When liquid water is heated and turns into water vapor.

exosphere   The area that includes all air beyond 120 miles above the earth.

Fahrenheit   Degrees (F) used for measuring temperature.

fault   A break in a rock formation caused by shifting of the earth's crust, along which movement can occur.

feldspar   Any of several crystalline minerals made up of aluminum silicates with sodium, potassium, or calcium; usually glassy and moderately hard.

flood plain   A plain along a river, formed from sediment deposited by floods.

fog   A large mass of water vapor condensed into fine particles near the earth's surface.

force   The cause that puts an object at rest or alters the motion of a moving object.

freezing point   The temperature at which a liquid freezes or becomes a solid. The freezing point of water is 32 degrees F.

friction   The resistance to motion of two moving objects or surfaces that touch.

frost   Frozen dew or vapor.

fulcrum   The support, or point of support, on which a lever turns in raising or moving something.

fungi (plural for fungus)   Plantlike organism that does not contain chlorophyll and cannot make its own food.

g-force   Gravitational force; a force of attraction between any objects because of their masses.

germinate   To sprout or cause to sprout, as from a spore, seed, or bud.

granite   A very hard crystal rock, gray to pink in color, consisting of feldspar, quartz, and smaller amounts of other minerals.

graphite   A soft, black luster form of carbon found in nature.

Greenwich Observatory   The oldest observatory in constant use marking the prime meridian; zero degree longitude.

Greenwich time Solar time of the meridian of Greenwich, England, used as the basis for standard time throughout most of the world. (Also called *universal time* or U.T.)

gyroscope A small, heavy wheel rotated at high speed on anti-friction bearings.

halite Native sodium chloride; rock salt.

hematite A brownish-red or black iron ore.

highs Areas of high pressure that normally bring dry weather.

hornblende A black rock-forming mineral.

humidity The amount of moisture in the form of water vapor contained in the air.

humus Brown or black substance formed from the partial decay of plant or animal (organic) matter.

hygrometer An instrument used to measure humidity.

hypothesis A possible answer to a question or possible solution to a problem.

inclined plane A surface that leans or slants.

inertia The tendency of matter to remain at rest, if at rest; or if moving, to keep moving in the same direction unless affected by some outside force.

inner ear A section of the ear that contains the balancing organ.

International date line An imaginary line drawn north and south through the Pacific Ocean, largely along the 180th meridian, where each calendar day begins at midnight.

ionosphere The layer of air from 60 to 120 miles up.

iron A white, malleable, metallic element that can be magnetized easily.

island Land mass with water all around it.

isobars Lines drawn on a weather map that join places of equal air pressure.

isoline A line on a map connecting points of equal densities.

isthmus A small piece of land that connects two larger pieces.

law of inertia Any matter at rest tries to stay at rest; any matter in motion moves in a straight line until affected by some outside force.

layering To grow a plant by bending down and partly covering a living plant with earth so that it may take root.

legend A brief description, or key, accompanying an illustration or map.

lever A device consisting of a bar turning about a fixed point; the **fulcrum**; using power at one point to apply force at a second point to lift or sustain a weight at a third point.

lime A white substance, calcium oxide, obtained by the action of heat on limestone, shales, and other materials containing calcium carbonate.

limestone Rock consisting mainly of calcium carbonate often composed of the organic remains of sea animals such as mollusk, coral, etc.

lines of latitude Lines drawn around the earth, parallel to the **equator**, on maps and globes. They are used to indicate distances and locate points on the earth's surface in relation to the equator.

lines of longitude   Lines drawn from north to south on maps and globes to indicate distances and locate points.

lows   Areas of low pressure that often bring wet weather.

lunar eclipse   When the moon is hidden by the shadow of the earth.

magnetic declination   The difference between true north and magnetic north.

magnetic deviation   The defection of a compass needle due to outside magnetic influences.

manganese   A grayish-white, metallic, chemical element, usually hard and brittle, which rusts like iron but is not magnetic.

marble   A hard crystal or granular metamorphic limestone, white and variously colored, and sometimes streaked or mottled.

mass   The amount of matter in a body as measured by its **inertia** in contrast with weight which is a measure of the gravitational force on the body.

mean   Designates an intermediate figure between two extremes and figuratively implies moderation.

median   The middle number or point in a series arranged in order of size.

membranes   A thin, soft, pliable sheet or layer, especially of animal or vegetable tissue, serving as a covering or lining.

meridian   A great circle of the earth passing through the geographical poles at any given point on the earth's surface.

metamorphic   Rock that has been changed by pressure, heat, or water to become more compact and crystalline.

mica   Any of a group of minerals that crystallize in thin, somewhat flexible, translucent or colored, easily separated layers resistant to heat and electricity.

middle   Refers to the point or part equally distant from either or all sides or extremities and may apply to space or time.

minerals   An inorganic substance occurring naturally in the earth and having a consistent and distinctive set of physical properties.

minutes   The sixtieth part of any of certain units; 1/60 of a degree of an arc.

molecule   The smallest particle of an element or compound that can exist in the free state, and still retain the characteristics of the element or compound.

momentum   The mass of a moving body multiplied by its velocity; the quantity of the motion of a moving body.

nadir   The point of the celestial sphere directly opposite the zenith and directly below the observer.

nerve endings   The free end of a nerve or nerve fiber.

neutral   A state at which a substance is neither **acid** nor **alkali**.

nimbus cloud   A rain-producing cloud.

nitrogen   A colorless, tasteless, odorless gaseous chemical element.

Northern Hemisphere   All areas of the earth's surface lying north of the equator.

olfactory Pertaining to the sense of smell.

organism A living animal or plant.

orientate a map To adjust to a specified direction.

oxidation Chemical change combining oxygen with another substance.

oxide Any compound that is made up of oxygen combined with one other element.

peninsula Land that is like an **island**, but is connected to other land at one end; land mass surrounded by water on three sides.

petiole The stalk of a leaf.

photosynthesis A food-making process where green plants combine energy from light with water and carbon dioxide to make food.

planet Any heavenly body that shines by reflected sunlight and revolves about the sun.

polarity The condition of being positive or negative with respect to some reference point.

potassium A soft, silver-white, waxlike, metallic, chemical element that oxidizes rapidly when exposed to air.

pressure Force exerted against an opposing body; thrust distributed over a surface.

prevailing winds The strongest, most frequent winds in an area.

prime meridian The meridian from which longitude is measured both east and west; zero degree longitude. It passes through Greenwich, England.

psychrometer An instrument with wet and dry bulb thermometers for measuring moisture in the air. The dry bulb indicates the temperature of the air, the wet bulb helps determine the relative humidity.

quartz A brilliant, hexagonally-crystalline mineral, silicon dioxide, occurring in abundance; most often in a colorless, transparent form.

radiate heat To send out heat in rays.

radiation The process in which energy, in the form of rays of light, heat, etc., is sent out through space.

reaction A return or opposing action, force, influence, etc.

relative humidity The amount of moisture in the air compared with the maximum amount of moisture that the air could hold at the same temperature, expressed in percentage.

San Andreas fault An active fault in the earth's crust extending northwest from southern California for about 600 miles.

sandstone A compound sedimentary rock made up largely of sand grains (mainly quartz) held together by silica, lime, etc.

saturated Having absorbed all that can be taken in.

scale of miles The proportion that a map bears to the thing that it represents; ratio between the dimensions of a representation and those of the object (a scale of 1 inch to 1 mile).

seconds 1/60 of a minute of angular measurement.

sedimentary Rock formed of fragments transported, usually by water, from their original place.

selenite A kind of gypsum occurring in crystals.

silica A hard, glassy mineral found in a variety of forms such as quartz, sand, and opal.

silicon A nonmetallic chemical element occurring in several forms, found always in combination, and more abundant in nature than any other element except oxygen.

sodium A soft, silver-white, alkaline metallic chemical element having a waxlike consistency.

solar eclipse When the moon moves between the earth and the sun, so that we cannot see the sun.

solar energy Energy produced by or coming from the sun.

soluble Something that can be dissolved or made into a solution.

solution A mixture of dissolved materials.

Southern Hemisphere All areas of the earth's surface south of the equator.

spore A single cell that can grow into a new plant.

stabilize To keep from changing or fluctuating.

star A heavenly body, like our sun, that is self-luminous.

starch A white tasteless, odorless food substance found in many vegetables.

static Not moving; at rest or inactive.

stereoscopic vision The ability to have depth perception. Each eye sees a slightly different view of the same object. Your brain coordinates the two views to form a three-dimensional image.

stethoscope A tube adapted for listening to the sounds produced in the body.

stimuli Agents which will provoke active reaction in a living organism.

stomata A microscopic opening in the leaves of plants, surrounded by guard cells, that allow the plant to breathe.

stratosphere The layer of air from 10 miles to 60 miles up.

stratus cloud A cloud extending in a long, low gray layer with an almost uniform base; often brings drizzle and can cover high ground and cause hill fog.

surface tension The pull of any liquid on its open surface so that the surface is as small as possible. The resulting concentration of molecules form a thin skin.

synclines Downward folds in stratified rock, from whose central axis the beds rise upward and outward in opposite directions; opposed to anticlines.

taste buds Any of the cells embedded in the tongue and functioning as the sense organs of taste.

taut Pulled or drawn tight.

tincture of iodine A diluted solution of iodine.

trade wind A wind that blows steadily toward the equator from the northeast in the tropics north of the equator and from the southeast in the tropics south of the equator.

transpiration   The loss of water vapor from a plant.

tropical rain forest   A dense, evergreen forest occupying a tropical region having abundant rainfall throughout the year.

troposphere   The layer of air from the earth to about 10 miles up.

tubers   A swollen underground stem.

updraft   An upward flow of air caused by **convection currents** or the up-wind side of mountains.

vacuum   A space empty of matter.

velocity   The rate of motion of an object in a particular direction.

volume   Space occupied by matter.

warm fronts   Boundaries between two different air masses caused when warm air pushes cold air away; usually means warmer weather.

zenith   A point in the sky directly overhead. A point directly opposite the **nadir**.

Index

Island, 473
Isobars, 473
Isolines, **66–68**, 473
Isthmus, 473
Ivy plant, 377–378

J

Jars:
 for ant colonies, 291–294
 for earthworms, 307–309
 for insect collecting,
  275–277
 for killing insects,
  272–274
 for making water
  fountains,
  446–448
 for relaxing insects,
  278–281
 for sprouting seeds,
  390–392

K

Kidneys, human, 339
Killing insects, jar for,
 272–274
Kites:
 bird, **418–422**
 bow, **412–417**

L

Larvae, ant, 288, 290
Latitude:
 degrees of, 18–20
 lines of, 5, **18–20**, 473
 minutes of, 18, 20

using North Star to find,
 25–28
Laundry detergent:
 dissolving eggs with,
  129–131
 functioning of, 125–128
Law of inertia, 473
Layering, 473
Layers, rock, 208–211
Leaves:
 falling of, **368–371**
 function of, **352–355**
 growing plants from,
  379–380
 moisture given off by,
  364–367
 parts of, 368–370
 preserving, **372–374**
Legends (map), 40–41, 43,
 473
Lever, 473
Ligaments, human, 337
Light:
 need of plants for,
  359–361
 response of plants to,
  362–363
 sprouting seeds, effect
  of, 391
Lime, 473
Limestone, 224, 473
Liver:
 fish, 314
 human, 338
Longitude:
 calculating, **14–17**
 degrees of, 14–17
 distance between lines
  of, 6, 8

finding lines of, 6–7,
 9–10
lines of, 3, 5, 474
measurement of, 6, 7
and prime meridian,
 6–8
Lows, 474
Lunar eclipse, 474
Lungs, human, 340

M

Magnesium, 229
Magnesium salts, 234
Magnetic declination, angle
 of, 55, 57, 474
Magnetic deviation, **53–54**,
 474
Magnetic North Pole,
 55–57
Magnetic variation, 55, 57,
 58–61
Manganese, 474
Map(s):
 density shown on, 62–68
 depression contour lines
  on, 35–37
 directions using, 49–50
 driving range, calculating
  by, **47–48**
 of earth, **3–5**
 elevation contour lines
  on, 31–34
 headings using, 58–61
 isolines on, 66–68
 legends on, 40–41, 43,
  473
 magnetic variation
  shown on, 58, 61

Vinegar:
    making salt with, 92–93
    testing chalk with,
        253–254
Vision, stereoscopic, 476
Volume, **79–81**, 477

W

Warm air, rising of,
    153–155
Warm fronts, 477
Washing soda:
    making bath salts with,
        121–124
    softening water with,
        115–117
Water:
    adding weight to,
        454–456
    in air, **200–202**
    changing hard water to
        soft, **115–117**
    chemicals in, 229

cycles of, 227, 229
evaporation, cooling by,
    173–175
expansion of freezing,
    180–181
flow and rotation of,
    451–453
and friction, **449–450**
for guppies, 315, 317
hardness of, **111–114,
    230–233**
and heat absorption,
    143–145
molecules of, **82–85**
pressure of, **434–436**
removing iodine from,
    89–91
rock breakage from
    freezing, 212–214
salt and volume of, 79–81
separating materials with,
    222–223
testing for minerals in,
    227–229

Water level, **440–442**
Water pressure:
    measuring, **443–445**
    and size of container,
        437–439
    and water level, 440
Water vapor:
    in air, 200–201
    as breath condensation
        in cold air, 178–179
    as fog, 197
    as humidity, 176–177
Weight:
    of atmosphere, **160–163**
    of compressed vs.
        normal air, **164–166**
    water, adding to,
        454–456
Wind tunnels, **423–424**

Z

Zenith, 477
Zones of atmosphere, 163

About The Guy Who Wrote This Book

A keen observer of nature and an avid follower of scientific advances, author Robert W. Wood injects his own special brand of fun into children's physics. His Physics for Kids series has been through 13 printings, and he has written more than a dozen other science books. His innovative work has been featured in major newspapers and magazines.